PEACE AND
GOOD

PEACE AND GOOD

FRANCISCAN MEDITATIONS OF THE GOSPELS

(Second Edition)

GEORGE V. SABOL, OFS

AMDG Books
Phoenix, Arizona

George V. Sabol, ofs, PhD
georgesabol.com
gvsAMDG@gmail.com

ISBNs:
979-8-218-11876-1 (softcover)
979-8-218-22279-6 (eBook)

Second Edition

Printed in the United States of America

Cover and Interior design: 1106 Design
Illustrations: Rev. Kevin F. Novack and Mary Esther Stewart, ofs

To those seeking the peace of the all-good God.

MORNING PRAYER

It is a good day Lord,
to be conscious of your presence to me
now and every moment.

I pray that I might be aware, and to acknowledge,
your presence throughout today.

I praise you, my Lord.
You are good.
You are holy.
You are truth.
You are my hope.
You are my fondest dream.
You are what I believe.
You are my love forever.

I thank you my God. You have blessed me beyond measure. I
am your lowly servant yet you cherish me as your child. I am
unworthy of your blessings. May I share my gifts with others
so that they, too, may know your generosity and your love.

I trust you Lord although I do not know where I am or where
I am going. Like a sheep, may I always follow you, and by
following you may others also find comfort in that way.

I do not love you as I should. Today may I often be aware of your
presence to me so that my love for you may grow to fill my very being.

Amen to the Father.

Amen to Jesus.

Amen to the Spirit of God.

PREFACE

In 2007, a friend gave me a book, *Notes for Meditation*, by W. E. Lutyens, Priest of the Oratory of the Good Shepherd. Soon after, I began to use that book for daily meditation. The book was printed in 1933 in London, England. The book is small and easily carried in a coat pocket and conducive to being taken along when traveling. There are a few handwritten notes in pencil made by a previous owner who may have been in a religious order. On the inside back cover is written: "For use in Chapel, Page 7" and on the inside cover sheet is a signed name dated 1934. I often wonder who the owners were in the 74 years before me, and how it came to America from England. But, I mostly wonder why my friend bought it, since at that time she was certainly not outwardly disposed to such a book, and what brought her to make it a gift to me. For I truly believe that it, like so much in life, is a gift of true mystery from God.

Lutyens' book follows the Church's liturgical calendar beginning with the First Sunday of Advent. The meditation for each day is presented on one page. Apparently, the author's intent was to *stimulate* rather than *educate*. Each daily meditation has a brief heading. That is followed by a scriptural reference. Then, each daily meditation is set in three sections: 1—a reflective narrative on the cited scripture; 2—an interpretive observation of the significance of the scripture to the world of Lutyens' time; and 3—an invitation to the reader to search the message of the scripture. Section 3 is often done in the form of questions. In Lutyens' words, "They are designed to stimulate the mind to devotion by suggestion."

In this book, I follow the same general format employed by Lutyens. Each daily meditation begins with a brief citation from scripture. Those are predominantly from the gospel of John, Saint Francis' favorite scripture. Section 1 is typically a commentary on the gospel passage. Section 2 is a narrative from the life of Saint Francis or Saint Clare or one of their followers that exemplifies the selected gospel citation. Section 3, like Lutyens, is an invitation, often using questions, to stimulate the mind and soul to devotion by meditating on the gospel message and the example of the little brother from Assisi, Saint Francis.

This collection of 100 meditations follows, to some extent, the progression of Saint Francis' conversion to Jesus Christ.

It is noted that the author has occasionally used imaginative interpretations of both scripture and Franciscan history. It has been said that imagination can lead us closer to the truth than history and recorded fact. Although I do not claim my imaginary interpretations to be fact, my hope is that they serve to stimulate the reader to their own spiritual imagination and greater devotion to their God.

ACKNOWLEDGMENT

The preparation of these mediations would not have been possible without two sources: scriptures from the Bible and the recorded accounts, both historic and contemporary, of Saint Francis and his followers.

The Franciscan Institute of Saint Bonaventure University brought awareness to me of the fullness of Saint Francis' life and that of his followers. As a result, that aroused my imagination as to their humanity and spirituality. I am indebted and grateful to the many lecturers at the Institute, especially Michael Cusato, ofm, Jean-Francois Godet-Calogeras, PhD, and Bill Short, ofm.

In the preparation of this book, I shared a few of my writings with some of the friars at the Casa Franciscana mission in Guaymas, Sonora, Mexico, who gave me encouragement, and I am deeply thankful to John Peterson, ofm; Ivo Toneck, ofm; and Martin Jose Ibarra Deluna, ofm, for their kind support. I also acknowledge the many authors of the tales of Saint Francis and his followers, from Thomas of Celano, ofm, to Murray Bodo, ofm, and many more. We all have been so richly enlightened by the works of these authors.

The preparation and completion of this book was not possible without the effort of many others. My wife, Joyce, prepared the Word product and made countless edits, but her greatest contribution is her loving support, encouragement and Franciscan spirit to see us through this. Mary Esther Stewart, ofs, performed an amazing edit, providing much-needed corrections and masterful suggestions. My dear friend Sherri Grona worked her magic in final word processing and incorporation of the art work. A delight to me is the incorporation of beautiful and meaningful illustrations by Mary Esther and Rev. Kevin F. Novack. I thank and bless them for being with me on this journey.

And finally I thank my children and grandchildren, who gave me cause to leave something of my imagination and hopefully inspiration of Franciscan spirituality to them.

Many thanks to all of my family and friends, and mostly to the Holy Spirit, for I could not have penned these words on my own.

TABLE OF CONTENTS

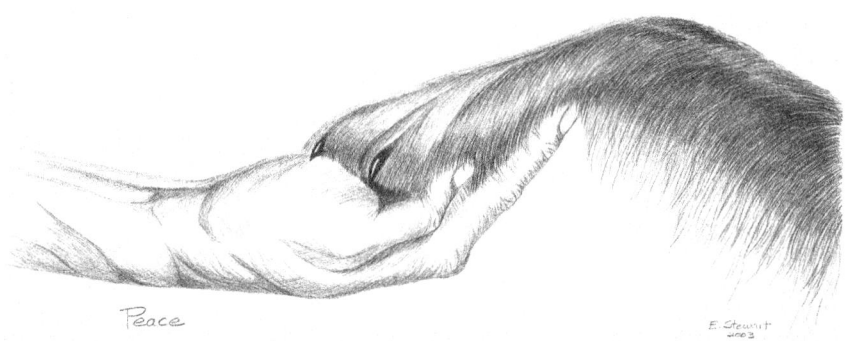

Peace

E. Stewart
2003

A THOUGHT OF GOD

In the beginning was the Word. The Word was
with God and the Word was God. —JOHN 1:1

1. The Word of God—Saint John, the beloved apostle and evangelist, uses an intimate approach to delve deeply into the nature of the divinity of Jesus that goes beyond His birth as the Son of God. Through John, we are told that Jesus exists intimately, one with God from the beginning and, through Jesus, all things came to be and are sustained. This is a willful thought of God brought to expression in this world by the Word of God, Jesus.

2. The Name of Francis—When Francis was born, his mother, Pica, first named him Giovanni, but his father, Pietro, who had been away, renamed him Francesco when he returned home from a merchant trip to France. It may have been prophetic of Pica to name him after John the Baptist as a new herald to the world of the King of Kings. And it may be fitting that Pietro, wishing his son to follow his will as a successful merchant, would give him a name to benefit his cloth business with connections in France.

3. A Thought of God—Pope Benedict XVI described the unimaginable mystery for us as an expression of God, "We are not some casual and meaningless product of evolution. Each of us is the result of the thought of God. Each of us is willed, each of us is loved, each of us is necessary." It should be comforting to know that each of us is the result of a loving plan and wisdom of God. There is a purpose for each of us that goes beyond the desires or plans of man. I but need to be attentive and receptive to what God calls me to be. Am I listening?

MESSENGERS

The person who does the will
of my Father in heaven. —Matt 7:21

1. Listen and Act—Jesus warned the people that it is not enough to listen to His words; it is also necessary to act upon them. The person that not only listens but also takes on the necessary service to God and man has built his house on rock and it will not fail.

2. Francis and the Poor Man—A poor man entered the cloth shop of Francis' father, begging for alms for the love of God. Francis, being occupied with business, did not assist the poor man with his needs. Later, he accused himself of rudeness to the poor man, saying to himself that if the beggar would have asked in the name of a great man of Assisi, how gracious he would have been. From then on Francis resolved not to deny a request of anyone asking in the name of God.

3. Life's Messengers—Jesus came at Christmas to be a messenger from God His Father. As a man, Jesus was a builder, and He knew the need of a solid foundation to build upon. Francis recognized that the poor man begging for alms was, in fact, a messenger from God, and if he was to build a solid foundation for his life, he needed to not only hear God's message but also to act upon it. Who have been the messengers in my life? Have I always been attentive to the messages and acted on them to serve God and man? Maybe more importantly, when do I need to be a messenger to others?

CANA WEDDING

THE INVITATION

Mary was at the wedding in Cana and Jesus and His
disciples had also been invited. —JOHN 2:1-2

1. Jesus Was Invited—Jesus was invited by many: the powerful and the weak, the rich and the poor, the faithful and the sinner. For this in His life, He was accused of being a glutton and friend of sinners. But those accusations only prove how completely Jesus embraced all human life. He was to redeem all of humanity, to cling to not only the souls of men but to their bodies as well. Everything that concerns us concerns Jesus, then as now.

2. Francis Was Invited—After Francis was released from prison as a result of Assisi's war with Perugia, he suffered much upon his return home. He wandered the streets, lost in anxiety of body, mind and spirit. His days were wandering in loneliness, and his nights filled with terror and waking in fright. Then, in that darkness of soul came a dream of a great lord's palace and a court with shields of victorious knights hung on the walls. When Francis asked what is this place, a voice announced, *"It is the court of the great knight Francis and of his followers."* From then, Francis embraced the message of the dream that set him in a direction of where he was to go. An invitation, as yet unclear, that he was to be a grand knight for the great Lord God and was to embrace countless men and women in following the way of Jesus.

3. I Am Invited—We all yearn for a sense of goal and purpose in life. It is not so much where I am or where I have been, as it is where am I going and where will I be in the days to come. We need to be going somewhere rather than going nowhere. It is the setting out that matters. For it is easier to change direction than to begin from a standstill. Where am I invited to go? What am I invited to do? What is the dream that I am to live? The only test to that invitation is: Can I invite Jesus to share the dream with me?

CANA WEDDING

THE PURPOSE

Mary said to Jesus, "They have no wine."
And Jesus replied, "What is that to me?" —JOHN 2:3-4

1. Mary's Purpose—As a woman, Mary was quick to notice the need of the wedding party, the pending embarrassment and anguish to those for which this was to be a day of joy and celebration. In her compassion for others and her eagerness for all to go well for others, Mary turned to Jesus with a tender hint. There was no request in what she said to her son. Did Mary then know of Jesus' power, of His concern for others? What did she really expect Him to do about the lack of wine? What was Mary's purpose? In Mary's concern Jesus found His purpose. In our need is the purpose of Jesus.

2. Francis' Purpose—After recovery from the war with Perugia, Francis left Assisi to join the papal army in the service of Pope Innocent III. His father, Pietro, had outfitted his son with armor and horse as a proper knight to win fame and glory for the family name. Then came the next dream, *"Francis, is it better to serve the Lord or the servant?"* Francis, in listening to the previous dream, had misinterpreted his purpose. He had tried to make God's will for him into his will for glory. Francis needed to look deeper into the invitation. He had started on his way but it was not Jesus' way. He turned back to Assisi in the humiliation of retreat. Francis returned from where he began in order to listen more closely for the tender hint of what the Lord's purpose was for him.

3. My Purpose—Surely, I have a purpose other than making the best of life's opportunities and chances that come my way. If so, I am nothing more than a helpless victim of circumstances, the whim of life's fortunes and not the master of my destiny. My life's goal is stability and peace of mind that where I am headed is where I am to be. We may not discern our purpose in dreams, but surely our Lord will send tender hints along the way if we but listen and see. My ears are but to listen to His voice and my eyes to see His face to know the Lord's purpose for me.

CANA WEDDING

THE DIRECTION

Mary said, "Do whatever he tells you." —John 2:5

1. Mary Knew—Mary, Jesus' mother, knew. Maybe mothers know the child better than the child will openly confess. She knew that Jesus would understand and honor her concern, not for herself, but for others. She turned to the servants and said to them, *"Do whatever he tells you."* Apparently, she was preparing them for what may be an unusual request by Jesus. It is interesting to wonder what sort of reaction she expected from Jesus. How far had Jesus gone in the past in helping others? What had Mary previously witnessed of her son? Regardless, Mary's direction to the servants stands today for us as the first and the best sermon ever preached in the name of Jesus—*"Do whatever He tells you."*

2. Francis Knew—After returning to Assisi, Francis entered a cave on Mount Subasio. It was there, in the darkness of body and soul that he prayed with deep intention. It was then that he was able to rid himself of the paralyzing fear of all that an unknown world, an unknown and unfulfilled life can offer. It was there that he found the courage to cry out, *"Oh God, who are you and what am I?"* It was in the cave that he began to hear the gentle whisper inside himself and he prayed more. The more he prayed, the stronger the whisper, and his heart burned with love. Francis knew and whispered back, *"I will do whatever you tell me."*

3. A Ready Heart—*"My heart is ready, oh Lord,"* is the cry from our cave. We have been prepared by all that went before us, our parents, our teachers, the Church, the communion of saints—ready your heart to listen and hear and obey. The Lord is calling to me in a gentle whisper to my heart. I must delve deeper into prayer so that I can shut out the inner fear and have the courage to say, *"Whatever you tell me Lord."*

CANA WEDDING

THE SERVICE

Fill the jars with water and take it to the steward. —JOHN 2:7

1. The Servant's Service—The servants at the wedding were the lowest, and to the gathering, the humblest of all. They waited on and served the guests as directed by others. Jesus directed them to fill the jars with water and they obeyed. They then took the jars to the steward of the wedding and likely, with trembling hands, served it to him. Certainly, to their surprise, the steward was gratified by their efforts. They were the first to learn that the water had been turned to finest wine. The servants had rescued the wedding feast! They were turned from the lowly to the humbly exalted. Where Jesus could have used angels, he chose instead to use men.

2. Franciscan Service—Francis, in yielding himself to God, became a servant to all. Francis, in humbling himself and embracing all creation as brothers and sisters, became a minister to all. The holy men and women down through the ages in following Francis and Clare are the jars of water turned to the finest wine poured out daily in serving and ministering to all. God, at all times, uses men and women to do His will. God chooses to use lowly men and women where He might have used angels and, in so doing, He takes the risk of their disobedience. The world has been blessed by those that listened and heard and obeyed the gentle whisper of the Lord. In their faith came the power to serve and the joy of following Jesus on the way.

3. My Service—All men and women are gifted by God to serve Him and so to serve all creation. As Christians we are baptized into service. We are confirmed with the gifts of the Holy Spirit to use those gifts for the betterment of others. We have the sacraments to nourish us and sustain us in life's work. God continues to use men and women where He could use angels. He takes the risk of our listening to His gentle whisper and of our obedience. Do I pray to hear His voice? Do I open my heart to His call? Do I open my life to His service?

CANA WEDDING

THE BEST WINE

You have kept the best wine till now. —JOHN 2:10

1. The Wedding Feast Wine—The steward did not know the source of the wine; he only knew that the wine was very good—the best. The servants knew not only the source of the wine, but they also knew something of the person of Jesus; they saw His work, His wonder, and the joy of it all. It was the gift from Jesus that brought that joy, and they were witnesses to that joy.

2. Lady Poverty—In the cave, Francis remembered the dream of the great lord's palace where a beautiful princess held court. He now knew that the lady of his dream was symbolic of the poor Jesus, and she was Lady Poverty. Lady Poverty filled him where before there was only emptiness. He was in love with the lovely lady, and to serve her was to fulfill his every dream, his every desire. Where there was sadness she brought joy, strength in weakness, softness to the hard, peace in conflict, beauty in the disfigured, and life in death. Francis knew that Lady Poverty was the grape crushed to yield the gift of the finest wine. The servant always knows.

3. My Gift of Finest Wine—Those that serve are nearest the master. Surely in my life the Master has asked me to fill the jar of my life with my gift and to draw out for others. The gift is freely given, not earned nor asked for, not for my benefit but for the good of others, maybe for the good and blessing of all. Small or great, the reward of the gift is the same, joy and peace and good for others. Do I open my heart to make room for my gift? Do I pray to know my gift? Do I stretch out my arms to give my gift to others? For truly, I have a gift from the Holy Spirit that no one else has in exactly the same manner.

GOD IS MINDFUL

The angel said, "Don't be afraid, Zechariah,
God has heard your prayer." —LUKE 1:13

1. Zechariah and the Angel—The name Zechariah means "God is mindful"
    in Hebrew. Zechariah was a priest in the Temple where he had given his
    life's work to serving God and His people. He and his wife, Elizabeth,
    had yet to conceive a child. By now Zechariah had lost hope and maybe
    even become a bit bitter at God for not having answered his prayer. Where
    was God to be found by a faithful servant? Perhaps that disappointment
    had settled strongly in his heart when the angel Gabriel announced that
    Elizabeth would bear him a son, and that led Zechariah to answer Gabriel
    with doubt and lack of faith.

2. Francis and His Mother—We know of Francis' father, Pietro di Bernardone,
    the successful cloth merchant of Assisi, but we know little of his mother,
    Pica. We do know that when Francis' father chained him and locked him
    in the cellar of their house to avoid Francis' further embarrassment to the
    family, Pica released him. Maybe Pietro had grown discontented with
    his son for rejecting the father's business. However, that disappointment
    turned to rage and violence against his son. But God remained mindful
    of Francis and Pica remained mindful of a mother's love for a son. Maybe
    Pica came to her son with a message such as Gabriel's to Zechariah, "Do
    not be afraid. I have heard your prayers."

3. Christmas—Christmas is a reminder that God is mindful of us. In the
    fullness of God's time He sent His son, Jesus, to be the bearer of the
    eternal message to us, "Do not be afraid." God remains mindful of us as
    Zechariah discovered, as Francis discovered, as we likewise have discov-
    ered. May Christmas be a reminder to us of the Son of God, His humble
    birth on earth, and His lasting daily presence among us, assuring each
    of us of our Father's mindfulness of us. May we remember that Jesus has
    truly set us free.

HUMBLE TRANSFORMATION

Jesus replied to John, "Leave it like this for now.
It is fitting that we should, in this way, do all
that righteousness demands." —MATT 3:15

1. The Baptism of Jesus—Jesus, the chosen of God, sent to transform the world, to lift man from the dust of life and to elevate each as a jewel to His Father, humbly accepted baptism by John's hands. Jesus, stripped of His outer garments, stepped into the cold water of the Jordan River and allowed John to pour open the flood gates to heaven.

2. Francis before the Bishop of Assisi—When Francis' father, Pietro, could no longer bear the humiliation of his son begging in the streets, shabby and unkempt, mocked by all, he dragged him before the bishop of Assisi. It was there that Francis had the courage to be humbled to the world. Francis stripped himself not only of his clothes but of his reliance on all that the world offered, and accepted God as his father and the giver of all life's needs. Humbly, Francis began the transformation of his life to God.

3. My Transformation—Humility is a pearl of great price. It can be received only when we make room in our hearts for God. Only the truly humble can experience and know God. We can learn humility by the acceptance of the humiliation of our repeated failures, our inabilities, and our weaknesses. It may be only then that we learn of our reliance on God. We must turn to God, be transformed. What occupies the center of my life? Do I make room for God? Am I willing to accept what may be His humbling presence?

GOD'S WILL BE DONE

You will find a baby wrapped in swaddling
clothes and lying in a manger. —LUKE 2:12

1. Heaven's Joy—At the birth of Jesus an angel of the Lord came to the shepherds and announced the good news, the joy of heaven. God's son, the savior of the world is born, and He can be found in a stable, in a manger wrapped in swaddling clothes. Suddenly a great multitude of angels appeared singing praises to God. There was joy in heaven, the Father's joy that His son was born and was wrapped in the fabric of man; held safe in the arms of Mary and Joseph.

2. Francis' Joy—Francis, once wearing fine clothes and after leaving his father at the home of the bishop, traveled in cheap clothes. A friend gave him an old tunic. He chalked a Greek tau on that tunic as a sign of his joy at belonging to God the Father. Later, as his followers would give Francis a new or better tunic, he would trade it with another who he would meet who had a poorer tunic than his. How like Jesus, Francis found the greatest joy in being robed in simplicity and humility. If Jesus, the Son of God, was clothed in such humility, then Francis, the child of God, would also find joy in being as Jesus was. Surely, there was joy in heaven and the Father's joy with Francis, wrapped in the new birth of one that followed Jesus.

3. True Joy—Heaven found joy in Jesus, the Son of God, doing the Father's will. Francis and the saints through the ages found joy in willing to do as Jesus did in this life, and the heavens again were joyful. True joy is not found in a momentary thrill of emotion but in a resolute purpose in wanting to do the will of God. Achieving that purpose, finding true joy, is in our acceptance of the graces to follow Jesus. And the angels of heaven will sing with joy.

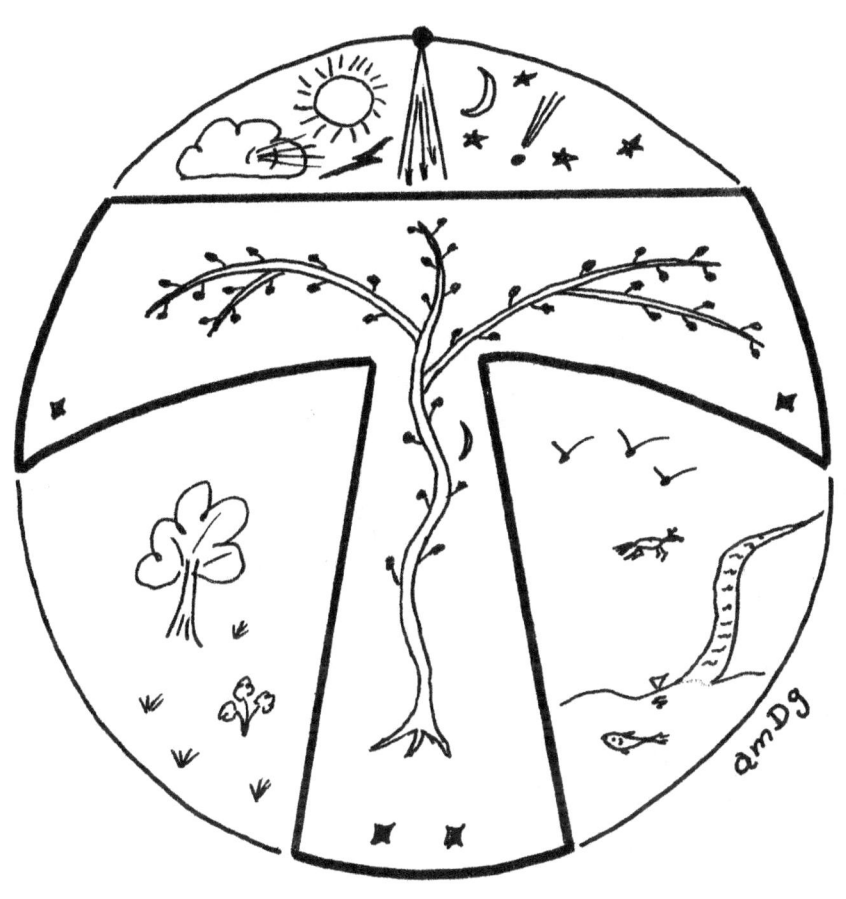

The Rule by Esther Stewart

GOD'S WISDOM

"Tell us," they asked Jesus, "are you the one John said was going to come, or should we expect someone else?" —MATT 11:2

1. John's Disciples Question Jesus—From prison, John the Baptist sent his disciples to ask this question of Jesus. Jesus responded as to what they hear of His words and see of His works. Jesus then went on to testify about John as being more than a prophet, and He concluded by stating that God's wisdom is shown to be true by its results.

2. Francis before the Pope—After Francis had 11 brothers he wrote a rule of life for them to follow. That rule relied mainly on words of the holy gospels. Then Francis and the brothers went to Rome to have the rule approved by Pope Innocent III. The pope questioned Francis about the harshness of their rule, especially the dire poverty and how they were to live. The pope instructed Francis to go and pray to the Lord with all of his heart to learn what is better and more beneficial to their souls. Francis withdrew to prayer and with the strength of God's grace, he returned to the pope with resolve to observe most holy poverty for their rule. Innocent III realized that Francis and his brothers were not proceeding according to human wisdom but rather according to the power and grace of the Holy Spirit, and he approved their way of life.

3. Divine Resolve—Life is wrought with questions and with consequences to our responses. How do we answer life's difficult questions? Where do we find the wisdom to make the best decisions? We often find counsel from good friends and family members, and we should seek advice from those who may have a better perspective than we have. But, more importantly, we need to withdraw in prayer and seek the grace to be open and receptive to the wisdom of God. If we trust and listen deep in our soul, then the results of our decisions will ring true by God's wisdom.

BARTIMAEUS

On the Road with Jesus

*On the way to Jerusalem near Jericho, a blind beggar
was sitting at the side of the road.* —LUKE 18:35

1. On the Road to Jerusalem—Jesus was returning one last time to Jerusalem.
    He had looked into the blind hearts of the Jewish leaders and knew their
    evil intent. He had seen the horrific violence of Roman law. He knew too
    well the road before Him. Blind Bartimaeus sat at the gate of Jericho,
    begging for his livelihood. Jewish custom branded him a sinner due to his
    blindness, and he was concerned with finding the means to live another
    day as he relied on the compassion of others. In his blindness, he did not
    know that on that day the compassion of God made flesh in man was on
    the road to him.

2. The Streets of Assisi—Francis, the son of Pietro di Bernardone, a successful
    cloth merchant, had made a fool of himself. He had given up his fine clothing
    for a ragged tunic and cord. Did he not see the spectacle that he had made
    of himself to the town? He was begging in the streets to buy rocks to repair
    the church of San Damiano, and there he was on the steps of the church of
    San Rufino calling to all as they entered or passed by, *"May God grant you
    peace."* Francis was in love with God and he wanted all to share that love;
    if he couldn't change them with his words then he would with his eyes.
    In the piazza and in the streets, mingled in the crowd were children and
    among them was a young girl, Clare, of a noble family. Clare saw Francis
    often and wondered what made him behave as he did. Was he crazy? But
    then, one day in front of her house, he picked up her shawl that she dropped
    and handed it to her and their eyes met. She did not hear what he said for
    she was captured by the peace and the compassion that she saw in his eyes.
    Later, she wondered what it would be like to have that compassion.

3. On the Road with Him—The cares of life can blind us to spiritual riches.
    We wake early to care for our duties and responsibilities, we struggle
    through the day to do what is ours to do and to be good servants, and we
    go to bed weary and spent. Such may be our life. But if so, what opportu-
    nities may we miss? What spiritual gifts are unseen? Jesus truly is on the
    road of life with us. Only through His eyes can we see life as He sees it.
    Only through Jesus can we see God.

BARTIMAEUS

THE BLIND BEGGAR

Bartimaeus, the son of Timaeus, heard that it was
Jesus of Nazareth passing by. —MARK 10:47

1. Bartimaeus Heard—Bartimaeus was sitting at the gate of Jericho on the
   road to Jerusalem. Suddenly, he heard the noise of the crowd leaving the
   city. He asked what was happening and was told that Jesus of Nazareth
   was passing by. Bartimaeus knew of Jesus, of His power and of His ability to cure. Immediately, he seized the opportunity. Now is the chance
   of a lifetime. He will not let that chance pass by. He steels himself with
   all of his courage.

2. Clare Heard—Clare heard the jeers of the people of Assisi. From her
   window, she could see Francis in the streets and at San Rufino. He was
   gentle; he was kind, even to those who made fun of him, including his
   brother Angelo who frequently mocked him. But Francis did not defend
   himself. He met their abuse with a gentle look and a nod as he wished
   them God's peace. Neither Clare's father nor her uncle would take such
   abuse from anyone. No, they would strike back harder than they received.
   Her parents told her what Francis said when he was before Bishop Guido
   was very wrong. Clare wondered if they had not looked into Francis' eyes
   as she had. Could they all be wrong? Was she wrong?

3. The Heart Hears—Amid the turmoil and clamor of life, of daily living,
   of earning our keep and of being good stewards to God, to our family, to
   our friends and to creation, lays the possibility of being on the wrong road,
   of not reading the signs and of missing the message. Jesus is on the road
   to us, but we need to, at least, be on the same road, if not traveling toward
   Him. What is my road? It certainly requires more than doing the right
   thing, for we can do that for all of the wrong reasons. To hear Jesus, to
   hear God's call above our mere existence requires that we listen with our
   heart. Do I take time to be quiet, to open my heart in prayer and adoration?
   Do I choose to seek God's grace through the sacraments, especially in the
   broken bread of His body and the wine outpoured of His blood? Jesus is
   on the road to me; He will answer if I just call. Do I have the courage to
   look into His eyes, for He is there just for me?

BARTIMAEUS

The Cry of Bartimaeus

Jesus of Nazareth, son of David, have pity on me. —Luke 18:38

1. Cry of Bartimaeus—Bartimaeus raised himself against the wall and turned toward the gate. The crowd noise was louder now. Jesus was near. He must be heard against the crowd noise. He can't let Jesus pass by without Him noticing him. He doesn't even know where Jesus is. But there is no holding back. With all of his might, with all of his ability, he yells above the crowd, *"Jesus of Nazareth, son of David, have mercy on me."*

2. Cry of Clare—Clare would often look for Francis in the street in front of her house or at San Rufino. She wanted to hear what he was saying. It was now more than a greeting of peace. He was now telling people of God's great love and how we are to seek God's kingdom and to serve the great King. She noticed that some people were now listening to him. She missed him when he was gone. It was said he lived in a cave and he stayed there for many days. She wondered what he found in the cave, and she began to dream of her cave where she could find the peace and compassion that Francis found. She was praying harder than she ever had, and in her prayers she would cry out in her heart, *"Francis help me, show me the way."*

3. Cry of the Heart—As Bartimaeus stood to shout out to Jesus, as Clare put herself where she could see Francis pointing to Jesus, what effort do I make to let my heart cry out to God to have mercy on me, to embrace me with His compassion, to be with Him and to look into His eyes of love? If I don't spend time in prayer, I will miss the signs on the road and Jesus may pass me by. What a pity that would be. There may be many roads home: Have I chosen the best road? Jesus is there to travel it with me. Let my heart lead the way.

BARTIMAEUS

THE CROWD

Those in front scolded Bartimaeus and
told him to be quiet. —LUKE 18:39

1. The Crowd—The crowd knew not of the real Jesus. He was a person of notoriety, a spectacle come to Jericho. They relished in the presence of such a person and it made them feel important to have Him in their city. For the moment, as if they could, they would possess Him and keep Him to their small, selfish interest. How dare the blind beggar, the sinner, shout out for His attention! He was theirs, was He not? Those in front tried to quiet Bartimaeus. But, with the cry of a drowning man Bartimaeus yelled all the louder, *"Jesus have mercy."*

2. Clare's Crowd—As Clare grew from a child to a young woman she received instructions from her family about her duties and responsibilities. She was from a noble family. They owned considerable property around Assisi and Perugia. She was to marry into another family similarly of nobility and property owners. The family was to grow stronger, more powerful. The merchant families like Francis' were growing too influential; they had too much money. Even now, there were problems in the Commune of Assisi between the noble families and the merchants. By now, Francis had a few followers from Assisi, even a priest was spending more time with Francis. The brothers, for that is how they called each other, enjoyed being together and found joy in their simple life. How can they be at such peace? They had given up all that they had. They now work at simple jobs to support themselves and live together where they can. Clare prayed harder, *"Jesus show me the way."*

3. Life's Crowd—Advent and Lent are the calls of the Church to break through our normal life with its distractions and false attractions. How, like the crowd to Bartimaeus, life tries to hush us to the voice of our heart. And, if we let it, we may no longer even hear our heart's cry. Advent and Lent are a time to pray hard, even to find ways as reminders through the day of which road we are to be on. As Jesus was on the road to Jerusalem and the cross when Bartimaeus encountered Him, so we will find Jesus on our spiritual way to Jerusalem. As Clare prayed for Jesus to show her the way, so shall we if we but shout all the louder.

BARTIMAEUS

TO BE SENT

Jesus stopped and said, "Bring him here." —MARK 10:49

1. Bartimaeus Was Sent—Jesus heard. It seems that He always heard the cry of the one above the noise of the many. He stopped and the crowd became still. He turned toward Bartimaeus, and the eyes of the crowd were on Jesus and on Bartimaeus. Silence fell. What was Jesus to do? Rather than going to Bartimaeus, He ordered those in front, those that had tried to quiet Bartimaeus, to bring him. They grabbed Bartimaeus by the arm, "Come, He calls you."

2. Clare was Sent—All had changed. Clare was a woman, past the time to be wed. Francis was preaching now, and on Palm Sunday of her eighteenth year, he was preaching from the pulpit of San Rufino. When he talked, it was as if he talked only to her, as if no one else existed, no one else in the church. Again, his brown eyes looked right into hers, reached deep into her heart. He was speaking to her alone, speaking of God's love and Jesus' love for us and how He said that we are to love one another. She trembled with joy and with fear; for that night under the cover of dark, she would leave her house. Francis' brothers would meet her and take her through the bishop's gate to the Portiuncula. She would join Francis and become the first sister in the little brotherhood with Francis. She would follow Francis' dream of poverty in rebuilding God's kingdom on earth.

3. We Are Sent—The world shouts at us to change life's circumstances so to find happiness, but the world cannot give us joy. During Advent and Lent, we are sent to discover joy in Christ, joy that the world cannot give. The Church beckons us to follow the road to joy much as Jesus took the road to Jerusalem, a road of His suffering for our unending joy. As Bartimaeus was sent by others; as Clare was sent by the brothers, the Church sends us to discover our joy, the joy of our heart, the joy of Jesus.

BARTIMAEUS

Not Held Back

Throwing off his cloak, Bartimaeus jumped
up and went to Jesus. —Mark 10:50

1. He Threw Off His Cloak—Bartimaeus could not be held back. Now was his chance. Nothing could stop him, nothing could hinder him, nothing could slow him down. He dropped his basket to the ground and cast off his cloak. He left all behind. Go to Jesus before He leaves, before He is lost in the crowd. Now, all else is nothing. To see again is worth it all.

2. Clare's Woolen Cloak—Clare was not held back. She embraced Lady Poverty as the brothers had before her. She cast off the cloak of nobility, the fine gown from her father's house much as Francis had cast off his father's clothes. Then, clothed in the poverty of Jesus in a woolen cloak with a rope around her waist, she stepped forward to the small altar of Saint Mary of the Angels. She knelt in sacrament as Francis took her long, beautiful, scented hair in his hands. Surely he paused as he looked down at Clare before him and with his brothers beside him, and prayed to God that what he was about to do was God's will and not his will. As the curls fell to the dirt floor of the chapel, Clare was wed in heart and soul to Jesus Christ and spiritually to Francis and the brotherhood for eternity.

3. My Sacrifice—Bartimaeus would not be held back in going to Jesus. Clare would sacrifice the entire world to gain the joy of union with God through the love of Jesus. Jesus' face was still turned to Jerusalem, the cross and the joy of the resurrection. What self-sacrifice for the love of God is calling to me? What am I to cast off that hinders me in answering that call? The end for Bartimaeus and Clare was joy. The end for Jesus is our joy. Love calls to us, and sacrifice is love doing its work.

BARTIMAEUS

LET ME SEE

Jesus said, "What do you want me to do for you?" He
replied, "Lord, let me have my sight back." —MATT 20:32-33

1. Jesus Asked—They brought Bartimaeus to Jesus. Surely Jesus knew what
   the blind man wanted. He had cured the blindness of others. Sight was
   always the request of the blind. To see was more valuable than all of the
   rest. *"Jesus, oh but to see again is all that I ask,"* was the plea of Bartimaeus.
   His eyes were opened. He looked up into the face of Jesus and at that
   moment knew Jesus.

2. Clare Asked—Clare had asked to join the brotherhood of Francis. Who
   was the intermediary? Was it Bishop Guido? She did not do this on her
   own, nor did Francis. She had looked into the eyes of Francis and her eyes
   had spoken as if to say, *"I want to see as you see."* And Francis' eyes spoke
   back as if to say, *"If it is the will of God it will be so."* With that act of the
   will, Clare entered the order of the lesser brothers and was forever bound
   in the mystery of spiritual love to God through Jesus and the brotherhood
   of Francis.

3. I Ask—Bartimaeus knew that he wanted to see again. Clare knew that
   she wanted to join Francis in doing the will of God. Jesus prayed not that
   His will be done, but that the cross be possible. When we simply turn
   toward God, then we begin to see clearly. With prayer, God becomes the
   object of our affection and the force in our life, then comes the power to
   do our will, and our will is then God's will.

BARTIMAEUS

To Follow Jesus

"Go, your faith has saved you." And Bartimaeus
followed Jesus along the road. —Mark 10:52

1. Bartimaeus Followed Jesus—Bartimaeus asked for sight and received more
   than he expected. Far more than his eyes were opened. He looked up into
   the eyes of Jesus and saw the face of mercy, the face of compassion, the
   face of God. Bartimaeus was saved for the asking, and he received more
   than he could imagine. He believed and he followed Jesus. Then he knew
   Jesus the man. Soon he was to learn of Jesus the Son of God. For the road
   to Jerusalem was to end in the glory of the risen Lord, the unexpected
   gift of eternal life.

2. Clare Followed Jesus—Clare had asked to join the brotherhood of Francis
   and it was God's will. From the Portiuncula she was taken by the brothers
   to a Benedictine monastery and later to the church of San Damiano. Soon
   her sister and mother and other women were to join Clare at San Damiano.
   Together, Francis and Clare, and the brothers and sisters showed the
   world the joy of the gospel. Today the little brothers and the poor sisters
   continue to point to Jesus of Nazareth, the Son of God and the Savior of
   the world as the source of our true joy and eternal peace.

3. We Follow Jesus—Our repeated failures, our inability to help ourselves,
   throw us back to our risen Lord, Jesus Christ. It is only through our failures and weaknesses that we are humbled, and only the humble will truly
   see and know God. Bartimaeus' blindness led him to follow Jesus. Clare
   humbled herself so that she could follow Jesus. Jesus humbled Himself to
   become man and accept death so that we could follow Him to the Father
   in heaven. What failures and inabilities do I have that can be turned to
   power to follow Jesus? How am I called to humble myself so that I can
   know God? To follow Jesus is worth it all.

THE MAGNIFICAT

My heart praises the Lord. —LUKE 1:46

1. Mary's Message to Elizabeth—Soon after conceiving Jesus by the Holy Spirit, Mary traveled about 70 miles from Nazareth to be with her cousin, Elizabeth, who was more than six months pregnant with John, later known as the Baptist. In that meeting of the two women, Luke captures the Magnificat of Mary. In that song, she poured out her praise of God, the joy of her soul. She was happy because of the great things that God had done for her. Mary may have prayed those words throughout her life before she shared them with Luke. She may have sung those words to her baby in Bethlehem, and Jesus may have heard this prayer of praise from his mother in their home in Nazareth.

2. Clare's Messages to Agnes—Clare lived as family with other women at San Damiano, searching for intimacy with Jesus. There, the Poor Ladies met with other women in a place where God was first, where they could share their love of God with others, and life was simple. Soon, others were to learn of the way of Clare and the Poor Ladies and wished to live as they did. One was Saint Agnes of Prague, the daughter of an earthly king and queen who, like Clare, refused the hand of royal courtiers. Clare and Agnes never met but they, like Mary and Elizabeth, poured out their love and praises of God. In one letter Clare, calling Agnes her sister, told Agnes that she is the spouse and the mother and the sister of her Lord. How like Mary and Elizabeth were Clare and Agnes to see the beauty of God deep within the womb of each other's souls.

3. Our Song of Praise—We too, like Mary and Clare, are called to let our hearts sing the praises of a God who has done great things for us. We are challenged to seek real wisdom, not the wisdom of the world, by bearing our gifts of the Holy Spirit to a world, a world that longs to know the greatness of God. Can we, like Mary, proclaim the Magnificat of our soul to others after Jesus humbly descends into the womb of our being, especially after receiving the sacrament of Holy Eucharist?

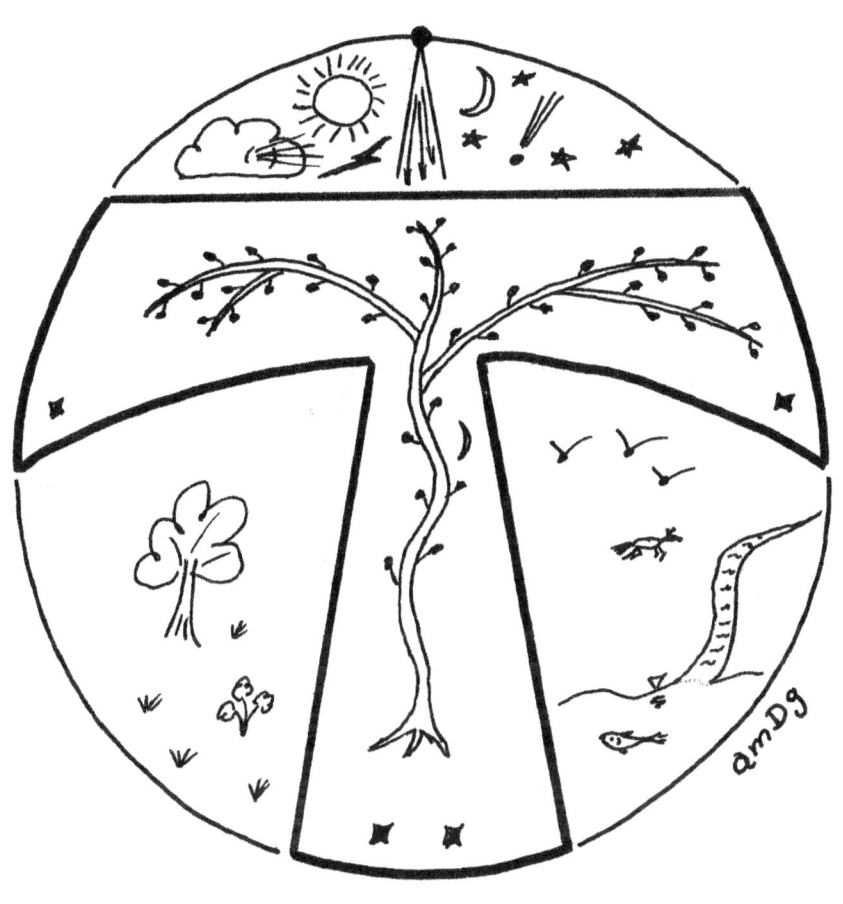

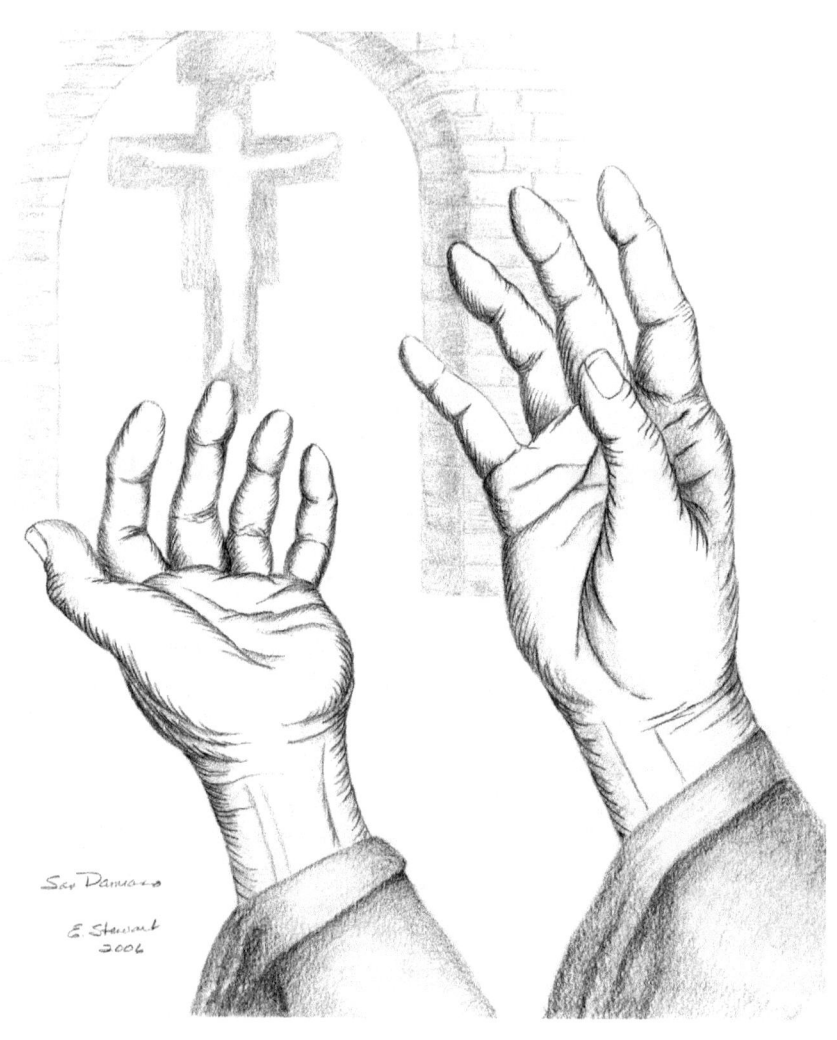

San Damiano by Esther Stewart

THE GREATEST COMMANDMENT

You must love the Lord your God with all your heart,
with all your soul, with all your mind, and
with all your strength. —Mark 12:30

1. A Son Speaks for His Father—That Jesus knew the Mosaic law and could capture the essence of the ten commandments into two rules is important but not surprising. What may be more relevant is that Jesus spoke not only as a divine son of God, but as a human son as well. Jesus spoke for His Father as a fully human son would speak for his father as a member of the family. Jesus spoke with pride and dignity as the son representing the Father.

2. A Son Petitions His Father—Saint Francis composed his *Prayer Before the Crucifix* early in his conversion and it is regarded as one of the first writings that we have by Francis. In that prayer, Francis petitions the most high glorious God to give him the spiritual dimensions of true faith, certain hope and perfect charity along with the human qualities of good sense and knowledge—all for the purpose of carrying out God's holy and true command. Francis, as a man, clung tenaciously to his divine sonship to his heavenly Father to grant the son's request. The beauty of the prayer is its simplicity. It is as a wise child would make a request of a parent, transitioning, from praise to petition to purpose. Truly Francis recognized his place in the family of God and God's role as the Father and his privileges as a son of God.

3. God Has His Rights—The first principle of the Ten Commandments is that there is but one God and there is to be no others. God, as the creator of the universe, has His rights, including the worship and glory given by all creatures. There remains to us as God's creation the necessity to worship our God. We are born with the prime objective to love and to worship God. If I desire and if I petition, my whole being can be an act of adoration to my creator. Do I, like Jesus, recognize and profess my sonship to the divine? Do I, like Francis, petition my heavenly Father with both praise and purpose? The Father has His rights, and as His children, we have ours.

THE GRACE OF GOD

A friend of tax collectors and sinners. —MATT 11:19

1. What Was Said of Jesus—In Matthew's gospel, Jesus speaks of what people in His day said of Him and of John the Baptist. The people complained that John was too austere and even possessed by evil. Then the same people said that Jesus led too indulgent a life, was a glutton and drunkard, a friend of tax collectors and sinners. In spite of those fickle criticisms by man, the will of God was proved right.

2. What Was Said of Francis—Those that knew the young Francis and left testimony describe him as good-natured and generous, a partygoer and singer of songs with his friends, lavish in spending and prodigal with time and money on feasts and other pleasures. But, when challenged for her son's action, his mother would reply, *"What do you think of my son? He will still be a son of God through grace."*

3. What Will Be Said of Me—If those that were witnesses of Jesus in His day could criticize Him, if Francis was prodigal and yet a saint, what may be said by others of me? And more importantly, what do I say about others, what is my judgment of them? None of us is called to be a reproduction of John the Baptist or Francis of Assisi, yet each is called to be a son or daughter of God. God's will for us will be proved right regardless of this world's judgment. The challenge for each of us is to say as did the mother of Francis, you and I will still be a son or daughter of God. All we need to do is say yes to the grace of God.

WHAT DOES JESUS SAY I AM?

THE QUESTION OF THE PEOPLE

Who do people say I am? —MATT 16:13

1. Jesus the Prophet—Jesus accepted the title of prophet from the people although He may not have claimed the title, preferring to refer to Himself as the Son of Man. But why not profess Himself as the Son of God, which is beyond being merely a prophet and far superior to being simply, as we, a son of man? For Jesus, having acknowledged divine incarnation, it was far more amazing to Him to express the marvel of God's divine love of us that He was, in fact and in all ways, a Son of Man. This scene, maybe more than any in the gospel, portrays Jesus much like us, asking what do others think of me? If so, Jesus the man shared with us our human feebleness and, at that time, supplanted His divinity.

2. Francis the Fool—Jesus' request of Francis to rebuild the church meant more than building with stones; it meant that Francis was to incarnate Jesus in his own person. He was to trust God completely and to abandon any reliance upon the world. To do so was to be a fool to the world. He had already left the world of his father, but how far was he to go to renew the world of God? To do so was to trust what he felt in his heart rather than what his mind and his experience would tell him. To trust all to his God he risked being a fool to many. For Francis, he was willing to take the risk of living as a son of God at the expense of his human nature as a son of man.

3. Jesus' Image of Me—Jesus took on humanity to give us the knowledge of God's divine nature. Francis set his humanity as second so as to live as a son of God. How like two friends passionately in love, each wanting to embrace the other in himself, molding himself into the image of the other. What is Jesus' image of me? How am I like unto Him? Can I but imagine what God says who I am? If I can imagine it, I can be it.

WHAT DOES JESUS SAY I AM?

THE QUESTION OF THE DISCIPLES

But you, who do you say I am? —MATT 16:15

1. **Peter's Response**—To Jesus' question Peter responded with all conviction; *"You are the Christ, the living son of God."* There is much about God that we cannot know in this life: God's power, God's majesty, God's eternal being. What was it that Peter saw in Jesus, not with his eyes but with his heart, that he could profess with all confidence of Jesus' oneness with God? Maybe there are some of us for whom seeing God's goodness is all that they need to know of God in this life! Was it Jesus' statement that only God is good that was the defining moment for Peter? Can it be that Peter saw nothing but good, the all-good in everything of Jesus? In Jesus' goodness was all that Peter needed for a conviction of a lifetime to know God.

2. **Francis' Response**—In the fall of 1224, on Mount LaVerna after the vision of the crucified Jesus and after receiving the impression of Jesus' wounds, Francis composed the *Praises of God*. In those praises Francis proclaimed the oneness of the holy Father and the King of heaven and earth as well as the Trinitarian Lord and God. Among the many names for God expressed by Francis is his clarion call that the Lord God is good, all-good, the highest good, living and true. Like Peter, Francis saw the goodness and beauty in his great and wonderful Lord, Almighty God and merciful Savior.

3. **My Response**—Knowing God's goodness is all that we need to know of God the Father, and that we see in the goodness of His son Jesus. Jesus is the character of God and the model for our character in this life. The measure of my goodness will be the measure of my Godlikeness. My response to Jesus' question must not only be that He is the Lord God but, more importantly, that others see goodness in me so that I reveal our good God to the world.

WHAT DOES JESUS SAY I AM?

JESUS CALLS SIMON THE ROCK

*You are Peter and on this rock I will
build my Church.* —MATT 16:18

1. The Making of Peter—In this act of Jesus He is not appointing a master builder for His Church, but rather is initiating the building of a master of a man to lead His church. Before this, and soon to end, was Peter the fisherman. Peter had neither the qualifications nor experience to lead Jesus' followers or to build an assembly of future followers from the world. In that single act of Jesus' confidence, He filled the sails of Peter's spirit with trust in the Lord that through him the Lord's will would be done. Little would Peter have been able to comprehend that the foundation laid by Jesus would be the beginning of a community of believers for eternity that he would lead for the Lord.

2. The Making of Francis—When Francis entered the deteriorating church of San Damiano outside of the walls of Assisi, he was filled with confusion and doubt. He had dreams and inner voices telling him that he was to be a knight with brave followers for the Lord. But how was he, the son of a merchant, with no resources or training, no qualifications for leading, to begin to make that dream come true? Then with his head lifted in prayer a voice came from the crucifix, *"Francis, repair my church, as you see, it is falling down."* His confusion and doubt were dispelled. At once, he could see that the church needed repair, and although he was not a builder, this was something that he could do. Immediately he set about removing the debris and setting stone upon stone to rebuild the old church. Soon other young men would ask what was he doing, and maybe his response was simply, *"Hand me a stone."* What Francis couldn't do, was not qualified to do, the Lord did through him and made Francis a builder of living stones. And those living stones are a renewed church.

3. The Lord's Making of Me—As Jesus gave Simon Peter what was needed to do God's will, and as Jesus gave Francis what was needed for Francis to be a builder of living stones, so too will Jesus surely give to each of us in turn what is needed for us to do God's will. Can we believe that not many but rather all are called, each in our own way, to do what God would have us do? Maybe there is one thing in this life that no one but I can do. Do I listen to the whisper of God? When I hear that whisper can I whisper weakly and feebly back to God, *"Yes, Lord"*? If so, I too am a living stone bound by the communion of saints in the temple of God's Kingdom.

WHAT DOES JESUS SAY I AM?

SALT AND LIGHT

You are the salt of the earth . . . You are the
light of the world. —MATT 5:13-14

1. Jesus' Image of Us—That Jesus saw His friends and followers as the salt of the earth and the light of the world speaks of His image of them. Not only were they good and desirable unto themselves, but more importantly, they would make all else good and desirable. Where there was complacency and dullness, they would bring the spice of life. Where there was fear and despair, they would bring true faith and eternal hope. More importantly, Jesus' image continues for each of us that we too are to be an example to the world, that seeing the goodness in us, here on earth, that we may come to know the goodness of the Father in heaven.

2. The Franciscan Image—Francis of Assisi bound himself to the power of Jesus so that Jesus' image of him would burn through all of the worldly condition, the human armor, the spiritual dullness, such that he would see the likeness of the Most High God in the radiance of the sun and the divine presence and splendor in the brightness of the moon. In binding himself to Jesus and binding himself to his companions, Francis bound all Franciscans to the virtue, to the power, and to the guidance of Jesus.

3. My Image—My every thought, my every desire, my every decision not only reflects what I am but what I will be. Hence the importance of critical self-examination. What is the path that I have placed myself on, and will it lead to the end that I desire for myself? Can I say of myself that I am a reflection of God's image of me? Can others say of me, at least occasionally, that I am the salt of the earth, the light of the world? The state of my soul is directed by my will. For what I long for, what I imagine, I become. What is my image of myself, and is it Jesus' image of what I am to be?

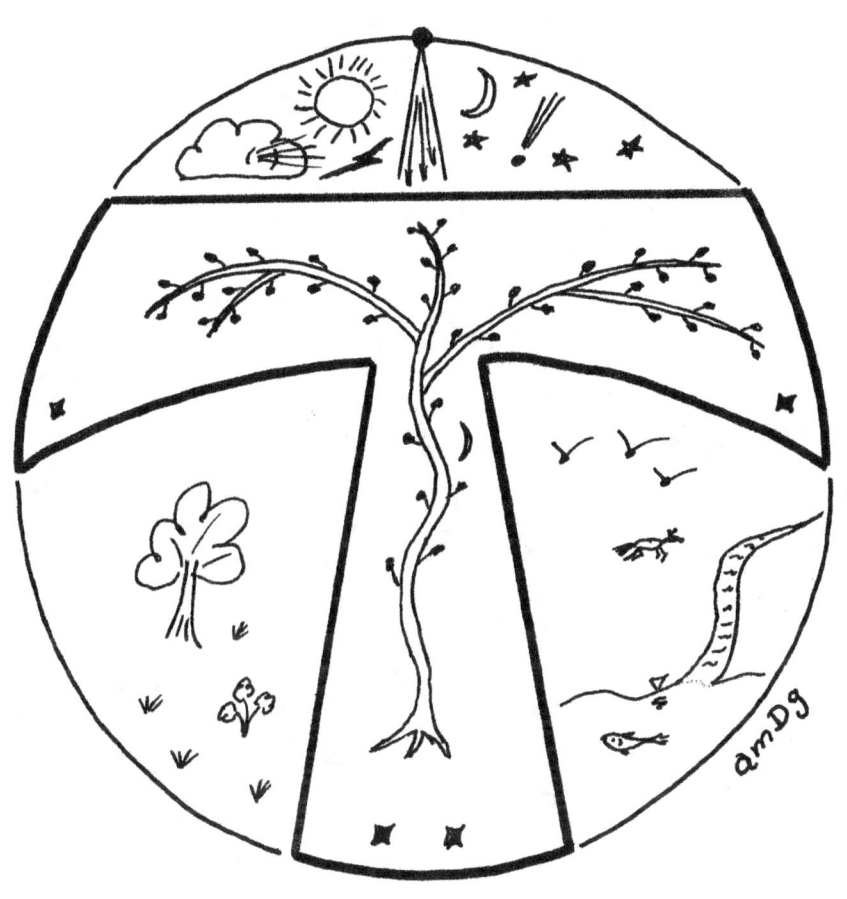

31

Vine and Branches by Kevin Novack

WHAT DOES JESUS SAY I AM?

BRANCHES

I am the vine, you are the branches. —JOHN 15:5

1. Jesus' Thoughts—In His teaching, Jesus used the simple things of life to speak of God. The daily scenes of life are drawn into His sacred conspiracy to capture us for His Father. Whether it was the image of the grapevine and its branches, or the birds and flowers of the field, or the hairs on our head, all speak of and point to a God of majesty that cares deeply for each of us. Jesus used these as a challenge to our senses and our mind to think of God, to think like God—all is good. Those who would listen, would ponder the words, would hold them in their hearts and would discover the truth of God. His words are a challenge: As we accept His words, God is revealed; as we reject His words, God is concealed.

2. Francis' Thoughts—Francis saw himself as a troubadour for the Lord, playing music with his life to please God and to draw others into a chorus of joy and praise. Was it the words of Jesus that caused Francis to pick up a branch from the forest and to play it like a violin, dancing with all of creation in joy for his discovery of the truth of Jesus' words, of the joy of God? In dwelling on the words of Jesus, Francis saw the world as a way to point to Jesus as the vine and to rejoice in being His branch.

3. My Thoughts—God made all things and all things point to God. Everything speaks of God and is to lead us to the discovery and knowledge of God. Can I, like Francis, hear the truths in the simple words of Jesus and come to know and love my God? Do I reflect the thoughts of Jesus for me and point to God for others? If I but think of beauty, simplicity, honesty, purity, virtue and the truth of Jesus and see it in this world, then I will think of heaven and sing as a troubadour for God.

WHAT DOES JESUS SAY I AM?

SONS OF GOD

You are the Sons of God —MATT 5:9

1. Happiness of Jesus—In the beatitudes Jesus spoke of happiness: those that are poor in spirit, are gentle, that mourn and give comfort, do what is right, are merciful, pure in heart, and are peacemakers. Jesus said that those are the sons of God, and the kingdom of heaven is theirs. Jesus used the beatitudes to teach the crowds, and a teacher can only teach what he knows. Although Jesus was teaching the source of true happiness and joy to the crowd, He was also plainly speaking of the source of joy within Himself. For Jesus' joy was but a reflection of the beatitudes within Him. For Jesus is the perfect Son of God and the kingdom of heaven is His.

2. Happiness of Francis—In the early days of the little brothers, they lived together at Rivotorto. At night they huddled together in the abandoned sty that was so small that Francis chalked names on the wood beams holding the roof so that each could have his place. Although either cold or hot, damp and windy, it was a palace of Lady Poverty to the brothers. Those were happy times for Francis and the brothers for they were living the beatitudes, living as Pope Francis would nearly 800 years later call the *Joy of the Gospels*.

3. Our Happiness—Happiness is a condition of our circumstances while joy is heartfelt. Our happiness, our joy, is in the acceptance and realization that we, too, are the sons of God and the kingdom of heaven is ours. For as a son is known by his likeness to his father, as a daughter is known by her learning from her mother, so are we to reflect the likeness and knowledge of the Father. How like the Father am I? Am I gentle and merciful? Do I do what is right and a peacemaker? Does my life reflect the beatitudes? When I do so, I am like Jesus, a son of God filled with happiness in my circumstances and filled with the joy of the Creator.

WHAT DOES JESUS SAY I AM?

FRIENDS

I call you friends. —JOHN 15:15

1. Jesus Chose Us—At the Last Supper Jesus said that He is the true vine and His Father is the vinedresser. To this He added the amazing declaration calling those with Him "friends," not that they chose Him but rather He chose them. And because He chose them, and they are His friends, they are to go out into the world and bear fruit from the vine.

2. Francis Called the Sultan Friend—Early in his conversion, Francis had wanted to be a martyr but had been thwarted several times in his attempts to go to the Holy Land. Moreover, Francis was not to serve God as a martyr for his faith, but rather to call the supposed enemy of the Church his friend and to live in exemplary fashion the final gospel command to love one another. When Francis and his companion, Illuminato, crossed the battle line at Damietta into the land of the Muslim army, it was not to be a martyr but rather to be an instrument of peace and to call the sultan "friend." We can but imagine the encounter of Francis with the sultan, but we can be certain that the two parted as friends, not as enemies.

3. Object of My Life—The object of a person's life is the pole round which our whole life revolves. Be it the object of power or peace, of enemy or friend, so is our life cast. As Jesus was to call Judas friend in the garden of Gethsemane and as Francis was to go to the sultan as an instrument of peace, what is the object of my life? As Jesus is the vine, do I invite the Father to trim me so as to bear good fruit? What am I to do today so that I can be the salt of the earth, the light of the world, to see myself as a son or daughter of God and to be joined with the friendship of God in the kingdom of heaven? For that I have been called by Jesus.

FINDING IN THE TEMPLE

THE TEMPLE

Every year His parents went to Jerusalem
for the feast of Passover. —LUKE 2:41

1. The Temple—Joseph and Mary along with the child Jesus would travel from Nazareth to Jerusalem for the Passover feast. As a child, Jesus would anticipate the adventure traveling the road with family and friends, gathering new and old companions along the way. The excitement, the memories would dance in His mind. They would arrive in Jerusalem filled with people and grand buildings: the palace, the Roman garrison, and most importantly, the temple. He knew of the temple built by Solomon and the new temple built by Herod. He dreamed of the God of Abraham and Moses, and of David in the Holy of Holies in that temple. He dreamed of His God and He dreamed of being with God in that temple.

2. The Gospel—As a boy, Francis would sometimes travel with his father on trips to France to buy cloth. Every trip beyond the walls of Assisi was an adventure, and the boy Francis dreamed of adventure as a knight on a powerful steed with shield and sword in hand. As a man, the journey changed for Francis, as did the dream. His dream now was a radical living of the gospel as Jesus lived it. For Francis the temple was the gospel. Once he had that dream, everything else pointed to Jesus, every road sign of life was the direction to the Father. If there was a fork in the road, he chose the narrow path because that was the way that he read the gospel. And at every fork, every decision to follow the gospel came with the paradox of joy.

3. Godlike—The young can have a childlike intimacy with many things; certainly it is natural to have that intimacy with parents and grandparents and others close to them, but it can even extend to toys and pets. That same childlike intimacy can also be with God, a natural acceptance and intimacy with God unfettered by the complexities and struggles of life. With time, that intimacy can diminish as we, ourselves are lost to the vagaries of life. What are my most intimate memories and dreams of God? They should grow like fruit on a tree. What dream of Jesus comes alive in my heart? What must I do to savor that dream, to recreate that intimacy, to let it grow into Godlike goodness in my life?

FINDING IN THE TEMPLE

THE WORD OF GOD

The boy Jesus stayed behind in Jerusalem. —LUKE 2:43

1. The Scrolls—While in Jerusalem, Jesus would sometimes be with Joseph and the men in the temple and sometimes with his mother and the women. As a child there was much to see. He marveled at the tapestries on the walls, the gold-gilded doors and the curtain before the holiest part of the temple, and He dreamed of God behind that curtain. As He grew, it was the words spoken by the rabbis, especially the words that were read from the scrolls of scripture, that captured Him. Oh, how He wanted to hear more, to learn more. There was so much of this God that He must understand. This was where He was to be—with His God.

2. The Bible—The word of God, especially the gospel, was the rule for Francis' life. For him, the gospel worked in any situation that he found himself. He would always return to the word of God to measure himself and to direct the ways of the brothers. When he and the first brothers composed their rule of life for presentation to Pope Innocent III, it was filled with the words of the gospel. Francis so loved the word of God that those words written in a book were sacred as was the book itself. So, he preached and taught others to have reverence for the written word of God.

3. The Word—As the beloved disciple Saint John wrote, Jesus is the Word— the living expression of God in this world. God, through the Word, will unfold Himself to those that seek. We know the other by living and being intimate with the other. It is the same with God. What am I doing to nourish the fruit of my tree to grow in knowledge and intimacy with God? Do I use the Word of God to nourish the fruit of my spirit? Do I, like Jesus and Saint Francis and all the saints, seek to be intimate with my God? To seek God is true wisdom and joy.

FINDING IN THE TEMPLE

JESUS WAITS FOR US

They failed to find Him and went back to
Jerusalem looking for Him. —LUKE 2:45

1. Mary and Joseph Sought Jesus—As a child, Jesus could travel with His
    father and the men or with His mother and the women. It was a day or
    so before Mary and Joseph discovered that He was not traveling with
    either. They searched the caravan and sought Him among family and
    friends. Not finding Him, they hurried back to Jerusalem and looked
    everywhere for Him.

2. The Brothers Sought Each Other—The Lesser Brothers, as Francis
    called his followers, were filled with brotherly love for one another. One
    of Francis' greatest concerns was that they would always remain a brother-
    hood. Francis believed that God was never closer to them than when they
    loved and cherished one another sincerely. They were as living stones laid
    upon the foundation of Jesus Christ. They gathered from every part of the
    world and burned with a flame of charity as the new disciples of Christ.
    As Thomas of Celano would write of them, *"There were chaste embraces,
    delightful affection, a holy kiss, sweet conversation, modest laughter, joyful looks,
    a clear eye, a supple spirit, a peaceable tongue, a mild answer, a single purpose,
    prompt obedience, and untiring hands."*

3. Jesus Waits—We may be blessed in this life with caring relationships,
    with successes and a good life, but still we seek. Where is the best of life?
    What dream in the deepest of our heart remains unfulfilled? Is the pres-
    ence of God in my life all that I want it to be? Is there more—with even
    greater reward? God is always waiting for us in the temple of His being.
    Jesus is always waiting for us in the temple of the Church. Do I seek the
    intimacy of Jesus where He is most readily found in the sacraments of
    the Church, especially in the Blessed Sacrament and in Reconciliation?
    Jesus waits just for me.

FINDING IN THE TEMPLE

LOOKING FOR GOD

*They found Him in the Temple listening
and asking questions.* —LUKE 2:46

1. The Quest by Jesus—Jesus knew the history of His nation and of God's promise, but the lure of the teaching in the temple was irresistible. He returned to the temple for three days, listening to the teachers, asking questions of them and answering their questions of Him. To learn more of His God was all that mattered; it was the very breath of His life.

2. The Quest by Francis—The quest by Francis and the brothers was the life of the gospels, especially the poverty of Jesus and those that were with Him. To have nowhere to claim as their own where they laid their head was to follow Jesus. The quest for Lady Poverty, to gain her hand, could only be won if there was love for one another. Francis would describe it as the love of a mother for a son and a son for a mother. They were to be living examples of the joy of the gospel, of the joy of loving God and loving one another. That shared dream, shared quest, shared love was the very breath of their life together.

3. My Quest—There may well be something for me in this life that no one other than me can do. That may well be true for all of us. What a challenge that presents to us. What is it that I am to do? What is my quest that will fulfill my every desire, my fondest dream? Am I seeking to do God's will? To do God's will may be no more than to be open to the road signs along the way and to desire to take the right path. Then, to simply trust that if we lost our way, we must only continue to seek. Jesus waits for us.

FINDING IN THE TEMPLE

WE ASK WHY OF GOD

Why have you done this to us? —Luke 2:48

1. Their Question—That Mary and Joseph suffered terribly in searching for Jesus is certain. To have lost someone that is cherished is painful. To lose a child is pain that cannot be imagined, and which most, mercifully, need not endure. For three days Jesus was not in their life. They did not see His face or hear His voice. He was not there to greet them with a smile, to tease Mary for something to eat, to be with Joseph, learning what a father is to teach a son. But their prayers were answered and there was their son before them. The pain vanished in a blink, but then quickly the memory of the searing pain and the question—why?

2. Francis' Question—Listening to the word of God, Francis was puzzled that Jesus chose to be with publicans, tax collectors, and sinners. He seemed to avoid the self-professed pious. There seemed to be a serious distinction for Jesus between the pious and the simple at heart. Piety may be something that is only external, to be put on, whereas the simple may reflect the goodness of the heart. Francis avoided piety and clung tenaciously to the simple—fearing that Jesus would choose not to be with them, and he would pray, *"Who are you oh glorious God, and what are we that you should have us?"*

3. God's Answer—The question of "why" was asked of Jesus as a boy by His mother and father, and the gospel has many questions asked of Jesus, mostly not answered directly. Today we continue to ask the question of why to God. We can look to answer that question in all that Jesus did and was and is; God is Jesus' father and God is my father. Saint Francis believed and showed that all creation points to God as father and mother to us. Our being with God is to be like a son, like a daughter: intimate, personal, caring and inspiring.

FINDING IN THE TEMPLE

LEARN TO SEE GOD

Why were you looking for me? —LUKE 2:49

1. In the Temple—Jesus responded in a manner that points to His human childhood. *"Why were you looking for me? Didn't you know that I was here?"* To Jesus, where else would He be? Already, His relationship to God is certain. In what other house would He be? As a man, to learn to be a builder, He was to live in Joseph's house and build alongside Joseph. As the Son of God, doing the Father's business, meant that He was to spend time in God's house. Jesus was exactly where He was meant to be at that time. Were the rabbis of His childhood in the temple when Jesus returned as a man? If so, did they remember the boy and ask in their hearts, *"Where have you been? We have been waiting for your return."*

2. In the World—To be a follower of Jesus is to be a learner like Jesus. To learn is to see and to do and to thrill with each experience. Jesus had made everything of life holy. Jesus had looked up at the same sun and moon in wonder, had been refreshed in the humble water of the Jordan, had been touched by the spirit of the wind, had trod and touched and held mother earth in His hands. If so, they all had been spiritualized and were alive with the breath of Jesus—and were forever our brothers and sisters. Francis embraced all creation and all creatures because they are holy and good and free and simple.

3. In the Church—All of life is holy. As God is holy, so are we to be holy. My purpose in life is to be holy. With God all things are possible. The Church offers me a path to nourish my holiness. Where am I looking for God? As the sons and daughters of God we are to be holy. Do I look to the Church for all that God offers along the way?

FINDING IN THE TEMPLE

JESUS IN NAZARETH

His mother stored all these things in her heart. —LUKE 2:51

1. Jesus Grew—The child Jesus went back to Nazareth and was subject to His parents, Joseph and Mary. He lived and worked and grew in strength of body, in wisdom of mind, in Godliness of soul. He was looked upon with favor by the men and women of Nazareth. He did well and lived a good life, but He did not lose the vision granted Him in the temple as a child. He never lost sight of His need to do His Father's business. The time would come for Him to return to Jerusalem, to the temple, for there He would complete the work that His Father had sent Him to do. And His mother, Mary, would need these memories stored in her heart for when Jesus would again be lost to her for another three days.

2. Francis Grew—From Francis' childlike dream of knighthood to his dream of Lady Poverty to his quest to rebuild the Church was a journey of life. That journey was not one to be traveled alone. Francis took with him all those that dreamed as he dreamed. He collected a flock of brothers and sisters that would be in love with God and in love with each other, servants one to another, to give to each nourishment in body and spirit, and solace to those in doubt and uncertainty, and embrace the lonely and the weak. Those brothers and sisters of Francis, together with Jesus, grew in spiritual strength, in wisdom of God, in Godliness of soul, and are looked upon with favor by men and women of all ages.

3. A Beginning—For all things there is a beginning. We build on little successes so that we can have bigger successes. Little failures prepare us for the inevitable larger failures. Jesus learned at Nazareth so that He could succeed on Calvary. Saint Francis struggled in the cave so that he could lead others through the world. The test for me in life from beginning to end is, *"Can I invite Jesus to join me?"* Can I today?

LET YOUR NETS OUT

LAUNCH OUT

He said to Simon, "Put out into deep water and
let out your nets for a catch." —LUKE 5:4

1. The Builder—Jesus called out that morning to James and John, to Peter and Andrew in their father's boat to pull out and cast again. Surely, they knew the carpenter builder from Nazareth. What does he know of fishing? Stack blocks to make a wall, yes, to fish, no! Why did they listen? What did Jesus say or how did He say it? What was the human touch, the mystery, that made them listen and respond? It was foolish to listen to such unqualified advice—but they did.

2. The Merchant's Son—Francis was the son of a successful cloth merchant in Assisi. He was a member of the growing class of wealthy business people, and not of the noble class. He sold cloth to the nobles and may have been considered upwardly mobile in Assisi. He had a bright future before him and desired to be a knight. Maybe he would marry a noble's daughter and have both money from his business and land due to his marriage. It would be foolish to listen to those internal doubts, those nagging questions. Why rebuild the old church of San Damiano? Francis was not a builder; he didn't know how. He would need others to show him how to build with stone, and he couldn't do it alone. And why should he reach out and help those pathetic lepers? Even the Church considered them dead. Why indeed? But he did.

3. Me and No One Else—In our life, we may be successful, we may be comfortable in what we do and bring benefit not only to ourselves but to the greater good of many. Do I occasionally feel a desire, a calling from deep inside for a change? Maybe to add to my life a service to others or a deeper prayer life, even to cast out into the deep? Am I challenged by my own thoughts that I am not qualified, that it would be foolish? I might fail and others would think me the fool. But maybe there is one thing that God wants to do through me and through no one else. Is it time for me to cast out into the deep? Will I?

LET YOUR NETS OUT

But If You Say So

> "Master," Simon replied, "we worked hard all
> night long and caught nothing, but if you say
> so, I will cast out the nets." —LUKE 5:5

1. Peter's Call—At first, Peter rejected Jesus' direction to put out again. He
   was the fisherman; his friend Jesus was a builder. Maybe Peter looked into
   the face of his friend, there was something in Jesus' eyes that quieted the
   protest, and maybe with a shrug of his shoulders and a smile Peter said, *"but
   if you say so."* Peter would have done it for none other than Jesus. For Peter,
   the moment of call from God had come; it came at Jesus' time. Peter and
   Jesus had been together, had developed a friendship; Peter knew of Jesus
   the man but did not yet know Jesus the Son of God. At that moment, it
   was as if both men had been on the beach walking toward each other: Peter
   unaware of where he was going, Jesus knowing full well of the encounter
   and what He would ask of His friend. Peter had only to look up and see
   the eyes of Jesus—and unknowingly nod, *"but if you say so."*

2. Francis' Call—How often had Francis walked the hills of Monte Subasio,
   or prayed in the Basilica of San Rufino, or sat in the Piazza del Comune,
   not realizing that Jesus was walking toward him? But on that day in the
   church of San Damiano he looked up into the eyes of Jesus and heard
   God's call to "rebuild my church." Yes, the old church needed rebuilding,
   the walls were crumbling and the roof was fallen in. But Francis was a cloth
   merchant, not a builder. There is something in those wide eyes of Jesus
   from the cross. He knows our limitations and weaknesses better than we
   do, and He knows that in our weakness we will find our strength through
   God's freely given grace. Francis could not have rebuilt the Church for
   and by anyone other than Jesus.

3. My Call—To follow Jesus is the adventure of a lifetime, it is the adventure
   of love. God appeals to our spirit to conquer what seems beyond us. Fear
   is of no use to the world or to Jesus. For Jesus and for us there is *No Fear*.
   Do I love Jesus enough to venture His call—to cast off into the deep, to
   build the kingdom of God? The worth is only known in the doing.

THE CENTURION

WHAT TO ASK FOR

Sir, I am not worthy to have you under my roof. —MATT 8:8

1. Centurion's Petition—The centurion was an officer of the Roman army, a soldier of an occupying force in Israel. He came to Jesus with a petition to heal his servant. He obviously had heard of Jesus' healing power, and that Jesus was a man of great moral integrity and impeccable reputation. He also was aware of his own status among the local people, which made him unworthy to have Jesus enter his house. But more importantly, he was a man of compassion and loyalty to a faithful servant, probably a dear friend that was suffering.

2. Francis' Petition—In the early years of Francis' conversion as he sought to discern his way of life, he composed a *Prayer Before the Crucifix* at San Damiano. He must have prayed it aloud with his brothers since his early companions recorded it. In that prayer, Francis petitioned the most high, glorious God to enlighten the darkness of his heart, and to give him true faith, certain hope, and perfect charity. He concluded the petition with the intent to use that grace to do God's will.

3. My Petition—What is the object of my desires? What is the goal for my way in this life? For what do I pray? Can I, like the centurion, admit my unworthiness for God to enter into me both physically in Holy Eucharist and spiritually? Do I, like Francis, ask God for the graces to do His will? There are times when we, too, must admit our unworthiness and the darkness of our hearts so that God can find room under the roof of our hearts for true faith, certain hope, and perfect charity.

THE CENTURION

JESUS THE SAVIOR OF MEN

Just give the word and my servant will be cured. —MATT 8:8

1. The Power of Words—The centurion knew the power of words. He gives an order and soldiers obey, even unto certain death. He receives orders and he carries them out, even to his death. He had heard, and he came to believe, in the authority that Jesus had, not the authority of this world, but more importantly of the spiritual world. Jesus had the authority, even the power, over life and death. Jesus had only to give the word and His command would be carried out. If Jesus were but to give the word his servant would be healed.

2. The Holy Name of Jesus—Saint Bernardine of Sienna was a 15th-century Franciscan priest who had a great devotion to the name of Jesus, in fact, to the sanctity of all spoken words. In his *Prayer to the Holy Name*, he gives the name of Jesus full glory, grace, love and strength. To the name, he attributes the medicine of souls and the healing of the sick. The symbol IHS, often seen on churches, alters and the sacred host, is attributed to Saint Bernardine and is from the Latin Iesus Hominum Salvator, Jesus the savior of men.

3. Speak Lord, I Am Listening—We may well come in prayer to petition the Lord for many requests in our life. We pray for our health and the well-being of our family and friends. We can ask for items that are needed and those that are not needed but desired. We even pray for favorable outcomes that are nothing more than transient pleasures. But how are we at petitions to be cured of what afflicts our soul rather than our bodies, of petitions for grace rather than goods, of petitions for cures of what separates us from God and our fellow man? The Lord is listening, I but need to have the courage to ask to be healed. Jesus is my savior.

THE CENTURION

AUTHORITY

For I am under authority myself, and have
soldiers under me. —MATT 8:9

1. The World's Authority—The centurion understood authority and he rejoiced in it. He was under the authority of others, and others were under his authority. He cherished order and discipline. Authority was the means to accomplish goals. Rome had great power; therefore, Rome had great authority. The world understood power and the centurion recognized the power that Jesus possessed.

2. Fraternal Authority—A few years before his death, Francis wrote a short letter on a piece of parchment for his dear friend and nearly constant companion, Brother Leo. Although Francis, the founder of the order, was in ways the superior to Leo, he wrote the letter as a mother speaking to her son. In the letter, Francis gave his permission for Leo to follow the footprint of his Lord God in whatever way it seems better to do it, and to do that with the blessing of the Lord God and with Francis' obedience over him. Possibly Leo had been seeking permission to travel or to temporarily part from Francis, for the letter ends with an invitation for Leo to return to him, *"for the sake of your soul or for some consolation."*

3. Spiritual Authority—The commandments of God are clear as to authority; there is a Lord God and nothing is to go before Him, and we are to honor our father and mother. Jesus was also clear as to authority, calling Himself the Lord and master and the disciples His servants, but He did that after having washed their feet. It is good to take example from both the centurion in recognizing the power and authority of Jesus, our Lord and God, and from Brother Francis in how to exert authority with compassion for the other. Where in my life do I need to acquiesce to my Lord God, and where do I need to be more fraternal in my relations with others?

THE CENTURION

POWER OF FAITH

Nowhere in Israel have I found faith like this. —MATT 8:10

1. Faith of the Centurion—What was it that produced the centurion's faith in Jesus? Was it the reports of Jesus' works and healings? Or maybe as a commander the centurion had learned to look more deeply into the character of those who he commanded and those who he was about to confront. Whatever the cause, he placed his faith in the person of Jesus. He placed his total and unabashed trust that Jesus could and would grant his request. And Jesus marveled at such faith.

2. The Faith of Clare—In 1240 the European emperor, Frederick II, in trying to impose his authority in Umbria, was intent on taking possession of the pro-papal city of Assisi. The church and monastery of San Damiano were outside of the city walls and unprotected. Clare saved the monastery and the city by throwing herself on the ground before the advancing horde, holding the Blessed Sacrament in a small box. She prayed for the Lord to save His servants from the troops that had already entered the monastery. Clare, the champion of faith, obtained the salvation of the sisters and the safety of the city. Jesus must have again marveled at such faith.

3. Faith in the Power of Christ—There are ample examples of the power of faith, the power of prayer. They may not be as dramatic as the cure of the centurion's servant or the saving of the city of Assisi, but what are the miracles of everyday life that occur unnoticed in my life? What is it that I have accomplished or achieved that cannot be attributed to merely human endeavor? Do I believe in the power of Christ, in the power of prayer? Do I cast my prayers with confidence to our Lord and savior? Do I give Jesus a chance to marvel at my faith? If I do, I will surely marvel at God's blessings in my life.

THE CANTICLE OF CREATURES

A New Creation

In the beginning was the Word: the Word was with
God and the Word was God. He was with God in the
beginning. Through Him all things came to be, not one
thing had its being but through Him and that life was
the light of men, a light that shines in the dark, a light
that darkness could not overpower. —JOHN 1:1-5

1. Praise of the Creator—A few years before his death and after having
received the marks of the crucified Christ Jesus, Francis composed his
Canticle of Creatures in his native Umbrian, beginning in this way: *Most
High, all-powerful, good Lord, Yours are the praises the glory and the honor,
and all blessing. To You alone, Most High, do they belong, and no human is
worthy to mention Your Name.* In the canticle, Francis gives glory to God
as the Creator of all creatures in a world as best understood by Francis at
that time. From the heavens of sun, moon and stars to the four elements
of matter: wind, water, fire and earth, Francis saw all of creation as good
from an all-good God.

2. In the Fullness of Time—Time is best defined as a measure of change:
change from sunrise to sunset, from seed to harvest, from birth to death.
As such, there can be no concept of time for the eternal God. But in our
way, in the fullness of our time, Jesus came to us and is with us today as
He was with creation in the beginning. And, through Him, all creation
came to be and have life in Him.

3. Continuing Creation—We are now in that ever-changing miracle of God's
creation; that is our place in time. It is right for us today to give praise,
glory and honor to our all-powerful, good God, as Francis did. Can we,
like Francis, recognize with all humility the goodness of God to us and
to all mankind? Goodness pours out of God as light into darkness. Do I
let that goodness create light in me? And, do I create goodness and light
for my brothers and sisters and for all creation?

Saint Francis by Kevin Novack

THE CANTICLE OF CREATURES

THE WAY

Many believed in His name when they saw the signs
that He gave, but Jesus knew them all and did not trust
Himself to them; He never needed evidence about any
man; He could tell what a man had in him. —JOHN 2:23-25

1. Our Way—*Praised be You, my Lord, with all Your creatures, especially Sir Brother Sun. Who is the day and through whom You give us light. And he is beautiful and radiant with great splendor; and he bears a likeness of You Most High One.* When Francis composed his *Canticle of Creatures,* he was suffering from an eye disease that produced discharge from his eyes and considerable pain. Moreover, light, especially bright sunlight, was very painful and discomforting to him. Due to that condition, Francis lived in darkness, often in a wattle hut at San Damiano near his cherished Clare who gave light to his spirit. It is remarkable that Francis would choose to start his song to the creature, Brother Sun, that caused him the most suffering. How like Francis to see the good in God's creation and to praise his Lord for Brother Sun. How unlike our way to seek God's relief from our torment rather than to open our heart to His grace.

2. God's Way—John, in his gospel, tells us that many believed in Jesus because of the miracles that He performed. But Jesus did not place His trust in them because He knew what was in their hearts. It would be natural, and very human, for Francis to pray for relief from his eye torment and he well may have prayed for that. It also is likely that Francis' dear brothers, including the miracle worker Saint Anthony, would have sent up prayers of petition for a cure, maybe even a miracle for beloved Francis. But there was no cure, no miracle for Francis. How like Francis to see so clearly that God's way is not always our way.

3. Miracles—Jesus performed many miracles, often for apparent unthankful recipients. It is a requirement for canonization by the Church to document miracles performed through the intercession of a saint, and Francis himself was the human source for many miracles. We, too, may well be the recipient of miracles that are unbeknown to us. How thankful are we for our miracles? Remember, a miracle is not always God doing our will, but rather us doing the will of God.

THE CANTICLE OF CREATURES

Light for the Way

I am the light of the world; anyone who follows me will not be walking in the dark; he will have the light of life. —John 8:12

1. Companions on the Way—*Praised be You, my Lord, through Sister Moon and the Stars. In heaven You formed them shining and precious and fair.* The moon has long been associated with lovers as has been the fate of star-struck lovers. Can it be that this verse is not only praise for Sister Moon and the stars but also a love sonnet for his dear Sister Clare? Francis used the Umbrian word "clarite" translated in English as "shining" or "light." Certainly Clare was, *"shining and precious and fair"* to Francis. Francis attracted and welcomed both men and women to his brotherhood with creation to pursue the Creator of life. Who are our companions along the way? Surely, we must have those that are shining and precious and fair along the way, or the way may be too difficult for us.

2. Heavenly Companions—Have we not gazed upon the moon and not brought to memory a loved one that has been called from this life? Those loved ones are companions to us on this way and have been hung in heaven for us to cling to and to be drawn upward into the heavens to join them in eternity. We have been given many heavenly companions. Who are our saints, those who have walked the way before us, that illumine the way for us? Do we ask those companions to be with us on our journey?

3. Light of the World—The world today, as it was in Francis' time, is wrought in fear, uncertainty and darkness of spirit. Nation is in competition with nation; God's peoples seek to destroy each other over how each practices his faith; there is social and economic injustice. We will continue to walk in darkness until we are willing to embrace the Creator's light and find love not only in the lovers' moon but in the brotherhood and sisterhood of all. Are we willing to walk in that light, or do we choose to stay in darkness?

THE CANTICLE OF CREATURES

PEACE

The wind blows wherever it pleases; you hear its sound, but you cannot tell where it comes from or where it is going. That is how it is with all who are born of the Spirit. —JOHN 3:8

1. Francis' Peace—*Praised be You, my Lord, through Brother Wind, and through the air, cloudy, and serene, and every kind of weather, through whom You give sustenance to Your creatures.* If there is one word that best represents Brother Francis to the world, it is peace. Even a popular peace prayer and songs of peace are attributed to Francis of Assisi, and rightfully so. Whether with his brothers and sisters, with the Church, or even with the sultan, he was a messenger of peace to the world. His greeting to all was, *"May the Lord give you peace."* Francis was peace and calm that brought comfort even to wild animals.

2. God's Grace—Wind is simply invisible air in motion with no shape or form. Usually we ignore it except when its breeze refreshes us or its fury disturbs us. God's grace, like the wind, surrounds and engulfs us. It is everywhere and totally present to us, it is given each day to each of us in our uniqueness and, like a breeze, it cannot be repeated or copied by another. God's Spirit sends its grace unseen to us to sustain our calm so that we in turn can bring peace to our world.

3. Our Peace—I, too, am born of the Spirit. I, like Francis, should greet all with the message of peace. I am called to be a grace-filled cloud, and blessings on the lives of others. Do I? I should be a gracious cloud turning bitterness and suffering into sweetness and joy, not a storm cloud emitting thunder of impatience and flashes of anger. Which cloud do I choose to be?

THE CANTICLE OF CREATURES

HUMANITY

He got up from table, removed His outer garment and, taking a towel, wrapped it round His waist; He then poured water into a basin and began to wash the disciples' feet and to wipe them with the towel He was wearing. —JOHN 13:4-5

1. Humanity of Francis—*Praised be You, my Lord, through Sister Water, who is very useful and humble, and precious and chaste.* The pivotal event for Francis in his conversion is recorded by him in his Testament. *"And the Lord Himself led me among them [the lepers] and I made mercy to them. And when I left them, what had seemed bitter to me was turned into sweetness of body and soul."* Although these words are usually translated as "showed mercy," they are as distinct as the difference is between "make love" and "show love." Francis, in his keen sense of humanity, the humanity of Christ whom he followed, made mercy on the lepers. Francis is so exquisitely human that he can even express this spiritual appetite in terms of bitterness and sweetness. Is it no wonder that in that humanity he could see in Sister Water not only its usefulness, but that it is humble, precious, and chaste?

2. Humanity of Jesus—Scripture is rich with examples of Jesus' humanity through imagery of water: the wedding feast at Cana, His baptism in the Jordan, the Samaritan woman at the well, washing of His disciples' feet, and from His side on Calvary there came blood and water. To quench our thirst, Jesus the man, in death gave everything to the Father and to us— His divinity in His blood and His humanity in water. In remembrance, water is added to wine at Mass to symbolize the humanity of Christ. To the divine, precious wine was added the human, humble water.

3. My Humanity—Can we, like Francis, praise that which is useful, humble, precious and chaste? Do I, like Jesus, quench the thirst of others usefully, humbly, preciously and purely? When all of creation is precious to me, I am precious to all creatures. When my intents are pure, I am trusted. Am I?

THE CANTICLE OF CREATURES

BLINDNESS

It is for judgment that I have come into this
world, so that those without sight may see and
those with sight turn blind. —John 9:39

1. Francis' Blindness—*Praised be You, my Lord, through Brother Fire, through whom You light the night, and he is beautiful and playful and robust and strong.* In his last few years, Francis suffered from an eye disease that caused him great suffering and near blindness. Early in 1226 he was forced under obedience to let himself be treated by a physician. Prior to the cauterization by a red-hot iron to burn from the corner of his eye to his ear, he prayed to brother fire, "*Be gracious to me in this hour; be courteous! For a long time I have loved you in the Lord. I pray the Great Lord who created you, to temper now your heat that I may bear your gentle burning.*" What affliction, what blindness, what painful recovery, what cross am I suffering? Can I, like Francis, call it my brother and even love it in the Lord? Do I pray that it be gentle and courteous to me?

2. Spiritual Blindness—It seems to be, and in fact is, our human condition to bear the unpleasant along with our joys. And there is no assurance that these will be balanced, nor fair. It may be that our afflictions are an opportunity to see more clearly. It may be wonderful to pass through this life with no pain, no loss, no crosses. But at what cost? How could we sympathize with the severely burned victim if we never felt the pain of burned flesh? How could we comfort the grieving lover if we never lost one dear to us? How could we offer our hand to another if we have not endured the dark night of the soul? For it is in our affliction that we can learn to see more clearly.

3. The Blind Shall See—It was at Fonte Colombo that Francis was treated for his blindness. In that little Chapel of Mary Magdalen, Francis marked the side of a window with a tau. Was it there that he prayed to brother fire? At that time Francis suffered much in body and spirit. We know that he was a man of prayer. Is that tau a reminder for us that we, too, shall see and be freed from our blindness—but only through the grace of an all-good God. Do we ask God for that grace daily?

THE CANTICLE OF CREATURES

SISTER MOTHER EARTH

In vain you get up earlier, and put off going to
bed, sweating to make a living, since He provides
for His beloved as they sleep. —PSALM 127:2

1. Gifts—*Praised be You, my Lord, through our Sister Mother Earth, who
   sustains and governs us, and who produces various fruit with colored flowers
   and herbs.* It is revealing that Francis saw Earth as mother as we do today.
   Maybe mankind in the depths of its mind and heart always knew Earth to
   be mother, the bearer of gifts, the one that nourishes and teaches. Francis
   knew all to be a gift, a gift from the Almighty Creator, as Mother Earth
   was such a gift from an all-good God. In his testament Francis recognized
   that the Lord even gave him his brothers, his sisters too, and all was a gift
   freely given to nourish his body, revelations to his mind, and joy for his soul.
   Francis gratefully accepted those gifts, and with the strength of a laborer,
   the dedication of a servant, the skill of a craftsman, and the enthusiasm
   of an artist, Francis refined and blessed those gifts and returned them to
   his maker.

2. Jesus as Gift—Jesus is the vine planted in the divine; He nourishes, He
   teaches. Jesus is the gift from the ultimate mother, Mother God. With the
   gift of the incarnate God, we, the branches, can bear much fruit. Separated
   from the vine we bear nothing.

3. My Gift—God's gifts to us are not ours for the distinction between
   mankind and mankind, but for the service of mankind to mankind and
   mankind to God. From God comes the gift of grace to serve, to nourish,
   to teach, to heal, to bless. How do I see my gifts? How do I use my gifts?
   Gifts freely given are to be freely given. The gift of grape from the vine is
   crushed and made into wine. The gift of wheat is ground and made into
   bread. The gift of wine and bread is blessed and becomes the Body and
   Blood of Christ. I am to be the gift to all. Am I?

THE CANTICLE OF CREATURES

BROTHERHOOD OF PEACE

In the evening of that same day, the first day
of the week, the doors were closed in the room
where the disciples were. —JOHN 20:19

1. Francis as a Messenger of Peace—*Praised be You, my Lord, through those who give pardon for Your love, and bear infirmity and tribulation. Blessed are those who endure in peace, for by You, Most High, they shall be crowned.* Francis wrote the verse on forgiveness as a means to end a bitter feud between the bishop and the mayor of Assisi. Francis recognized that forgiveness, peace, and brotherhood belong together. One cannot exist without the others. There can be no brotherhood and no forgiveness unless there is peace in the hearts and that peace is offered to all. In his testament, Francis tells that the Lord revealed a greeting to him, *"May the Lord give you peace."*

2. Jesus as a Messenger of Peace—There are many examples of Jesus' greeting of peace, but none is more poignant than that to His apostles and especially to Thomas. For Thomas' lack of faith, Jesus freely gave peace and forgiveness with conviction, without recrimination and with no offense taken. Jesus surely wanted Thomas to be at peace. Christ is the Prince of Peace and His cross is the standard of forgiveness, *"They know not what they do."*

3. I Am to Be a Messenger of Peace—*"As I forgive"* is the condition and test of God's forgiveness of me, pronounced with each Lord's Prayer—solemnly proclaimed, not glibly spoken. It is binding on my soul in measure to how I bind my brother and sister. Am I at peace with all and with creation? I must be if I am to be at peace with God and forgiven by Him.

THE CANTICLE OF CREATURES

GOD'S PURPOSE

As the Father sent me, so am I sending you. —JOHN 20:21

1. Francis' Call—*Praised be You, Lord, for our Sister Bodily Death, from whom no one living may escape. Woe to those who die in mortal sin. Blessed are those whom death will find in Your Most Holy will; for the second death shall do them no harm.* Before Francis died, he said that he had done what was his to do. We may wonder if his thoughts were on his many successes: founding an order, or his miracles, or his rise in the Church, or his charismatic appeal by the people. Probably none of these were the essence of what he considered his calling. Rather, he answered the call to follow Jesus and to do the Father's work. And the Father's work is to love. Love demands all. From his conversion to his death, Francis' life was not his own. For Francis discovered the secret of this mystic life—love, love of the Creator and His creation. Surely Francis was lovingly found in the Father's Holy will.

2. Jesus' Call to Us—Jesus was sent in an act of love by the Father to return all of creation to a state of love. Jesus' work was love in His life and through His death so that we can have no fear of Sister Death. As Jesus worked, so shall we work. As Jesus was sent, so we are sent. As Jesus loved, so are we to love. We are all called, and we will all draw grace from the Holy Spirit to do the Father's work. For God is love.

3. Our Answer—As for Jesus, as for Francis, we, too, are bound to this mortal life. We can but find our way as we will it. Love, too, is an act of the will. The bonds of love will hold us to the right path though we may not know where that path leads. How we choose to love, how we bond our will to love is the test, so that we too can say, *"I have done what was mine to do."*

THE CANTICLE OF CREATURES

PRAISE, THANKS, AND SERVICE

One of his disciples said, "Lord, teach us to pray,
just as John taught his disciples." —LUKE 11:1

1. Francis Points to God in Prayer—*O praise and bless my Lord. Thank Him and serve Him, humbly but grandly!* Francis sang his canticle in praise of all that is beyond his world: the sun, moon and stars. Then he praised the four worldly elements: air, water, fire and earth. Finally, he praised mortal brotherhood through suffering and death. In his last stanza, Francis simply summarizes his way as best that he could follow Jesus. Love sees the majesty, the glory, the beauty, and the goodness of God in all creation and in all of human life. From that love springs unending praise of God and true joy. And joy brings spontaneous thanksgiving to the author of all goodness. With true thanksgiving comes the grace to serve, and humbly serve, both God and mankind.

2. Jesus Looks to His Father in Prayer—Jesus spent days under the radiance of the sun and nights with the moon and stars alone with His Father, our God. Jesus' joy was to praise and bless the Father. As air, water, fire and all earth were natural to Jesus, so all were a continuous reminder of the natural blessings from the Father. Jesus would cry out His thanks to the Father in praise and blessings. It was the sheer joy of being in the presence of His Father in the majesty of all creation that Jesus sought. Jesus prayed not to alter the will of God but to serve God, and to serve God in the humility of mortal man and in the grandness of God.

3. God Waits for Us in Our Prayer—If we can but see the beauty of God, the beauty, not only in all of His creation, but also the beauty of God where we must look, deep inside—deep into the leper that waits for our embrace. Love that sees the beauty of God sees the majesty, the glory, the holiness of God and His creation. Then pure prayer springs forth from the heart of love—for no other purpose than to be one with our God. God gives all to us and waits for us to be one with Him.

GOD'S GRACE IS PEACE

The angel came to her and said, "Peace be with you. The
Lord is with you and greatly blessed you." —LUKE 1:28

1. The Immaculate Conception—The angel Gabriel proclaimed to Mary
    that God had sanctified her so that no sin would touch her soul. Her
    womb would be a pure dwelling for the incarnate Son of God. On the
    feast of the Immaculate Conception, the Church uses the gospel of the
    Annunciation. That story of God's angel coming to Mary embodies the
    eternal hope and trust that God's grace triumphs over all else, for there
    is nothing that God cannot do.

2. An Instrument of Peace—In his *Testament*, Saint Francis wrote, *"The Lord
    revealed a greeting to me that we should say, 'May the Lord give you peace.'"*
    As Gabriel greeted Mary, so Francis admonished his followers to greet all
    with the blessing of God's peace. To live according to the pattern of the
    Holy Gospel, we are to be a people of peace, to be instruments of peace
    in a world of strife, turmoil and violence.

3. Trust God's Grace—It is easy for world events to unsettle our trust in
    God's grace. If those events greatly trouble us and cause us to fall prey
    to spiritual attack, maybe it is because we are failing to be instruments
    of God's peace. Maybe it is time to dwell upon the words of Gabriel to a
    frightened and unsettled Mary. Maybe it is time to listen to Saint Francis'
    admonition to greet all with the Lord's peace. The message is clear: Jesus
    triumphed over fear of death, God triumphs over evil. The answer of God's
    peace lies in persistent prayer and the grace of God.

RULE OF LIFE

My Father goes on working and so do I. —JOHN 5:17

1. God's Work—After Jesus cured the man at the pool of Bethzatha, some questioned Jesus about curing the man on the sabbath. Jesus' answer was simply that His Father continues to work and so must He. The priority for Jesus was the person in the here and now. It was necessary to do the Father's work, not man's bidding.

2. Francis' Work—Among the accomplishments of Francis and the early brothers was the writing of their *Rule of Life*. After years of struggle, that work was completed at Fonte Colombo (the fountain of the doves) and the rule was approved by Pope Honorius III on 29 November 1223. That rule was contrary to the existing norm for the Church and for society, and it gave birth to a new movement in the Church and throughout the world that continues today nearly 800 years later. For Francis and the brothers that way of life was a dream for a future that they believed in; a dream that was possible and became viable through the work of human hands and reality through the grace of God. For the brothers, and ultimately the sisters that followed Francis, it was and continues to be a vision of life through a commitment to the joy of the gospel and an ongoing opportunity to conversion to God's will.

3. My Work—As the Father works and Jesus works and Francis worked, so are we called to work in this way of life. As the development of the *Rule of Life* was a work of many hands, so shall our search to carry out God's will be the work of our hands. That work is best performed in the context of the community of the Church, the society that we function in, and the greater benefit of a good world. How am I called to work as Jesus did to cure the cripple at the pool, or to work as Francis did to bring to fruition a dream for a better way of life?

GIFTS

They brought out their gifts of gold, frankincense, and
myrrh and presented them to Him. —MATT 2:11

1. Three Gifts from the Wise Men—When the three astronomers from
   the east entered the house and saw the child with His mother, Mary,
   they knelt down and worshipped Him. Then each presented Him with a
   gift: gold for a King, frankincense for a God, myrrh for a man. It wasn't
   earthly wisdom or their knowledge of the stars that set them searching
   for the newborn babe. It was the grace of God that opened their minds
   to the possibility, and the grace of God that sustained and guided them,
   and the grace of God that enlightened them to the reality of God in the
   simplicity and humility of an infant child.

2. Three Gifts from Francis of Assisi—Through the grace of God, Francis
   was successful in founding the order of lesser brothers (Ordo Fratres
   Minores). With that, single men were able to dedicate their lives to God
   by proclaiming the gospel message to the world in poverty and humility.
   But Francis' vision for a radical change to the Church would not stop with
   men. In Francis' life he is also the cornerstone, through Saint Clare, of the
   order of poor ladies (Ordo Sanctae Clarae) for women, and the order of
   secular Franciscans (Ordo Franciscanus Secularis) for men and women,
   married or single. Of all that Francis accomplished, the greatest to the
   world, to the Church, and to countless men and women through the ages
   is being welcomed into the Franciscan family, one together in spirit and
   peace, uniting all as brothers and sisters of Jesus Christ and of all creation.
   Truly his rebuilding the Church has been a gift to the world.

3. My Gift—What will be my legacy? How will my time on earth be judged?
   As the star pointed the way to Jesus for the Wise Men, as the angels
   pointed the way to Bethlehem for the shepherds, as Francis pointed the
   way to Jesus for all men and women, as the saints pointed to Jesus with
   their words and lives, as those before us, our parents and grandparents
   pointed to Jesus, so are we with our lives to point to Jesus. Our legacy, how
   we will be judged, is how well did we point to Jesus? What will be my gift
   to God, to the world? It is to be more precious than gold, or frankincense
   or myrrh. My gift can be as simple as pointing the way to those with me
   as brothers and sisters in God's universe.

THE STORM

PRAYER

He went up into the hills to pray. —MATT 14:23

1. Time to Pray—After feeding the multitude with five loaves and two fish and having sent the disciples off in a boat, Jesus went into the hills to be alone with His Father and pray. That Jesus went off alone for prayer is often told in the gospels. Before a decisive event or after some great work, the gospels tell that Jesus drew apart into the hills to pray. That Jesus needed to be alone in prayer in preparation for His work or to reflect with His Father after His work was done is noteworthy unto itself.

2. Not Alone in Prayer—On the night that Clare left home to join Francis and the brothers at the Portiuncula, she surely prayed alone in her room with trembling fear and resolute hope. She was about to embark on a venture that would rend her family and be a scandal to Assisi. With no other recourse, she would lay her fate at the feet of Jesus. At the Portiuncula, Francis and the brothers prayed for Clare and for the faith and courage that this decisive event that was about to unfold was truly the will of God. Guido, the bishop of Assisi, prayed that God's will be done that night. Clare's prayer, Francis' prayer, the brothers' prayer, and Guido's prayer, all rose in a chorus that all heaven and all creation joined in. And the prayer of Clare and the Poor Ladies has never stopped. For when we pray, we never pray alone.

3. To See God—Blessed are the pure of heart for they shall see God. We can, and must, pray privately and publicly to our God. We should meditate on the words and life of Jesus. But to experience God fully is to draw off apart from others and to be alone in contemplation of God. To see God in our heart and not in our mind is the highest objective of spiritual life. That is the prayer of Jesus and of the saints, to be with God and thus to see God. Such purity in prayer is within the reach of all when we, like Saint Francis and Saint Clare, first seek to be simple, humble and pure. Not only to be humble and pure in deed, but to be simple in motive of the heart, and desire nothing but that which is good. God alone can set us free to be simple, humble and pure—if we but ask.

THE STORM

Alone with God

The boat was battling with a heavy sea. —Matt 14:24

1. The Storm—Jesus sent the disciples on in the boat while He stayed behind to pray. How He was to join them, or if He was, is not mentioned. As darkness fell, a sudden and severe storm beat upon the boat with fierce wind and waves to threaten them. They were alone and in great danger. They were doing what they could to save themselves against a force stronger than them.

2. The Town of Gubbio—The legend of the wolf of Gubbio in the *Little Flowers of Saint Francis* is akin to the storm on the sea. At the time, the town of Gubbio was being ravished by a very big wolf, fearsome and ferocious, which devoured not only animals but even humans. The citizens were in great fear and would only venture beyond the walls if armed as if going to battle. But those alone, even with their defenses, were unable to defend themselves against the wolf. Finally, no one dared to leave the town out of fear of the wolf.

3. Dark Times—Both the gospel of the storm on the sea and the legend of the wolf of Gubbio are allegories of life without God. Storms of life beat upon us and fears overwhelm us that are too much to handle on our own. Life has its dark times, and they come without warning and may come regardless of our best efforts to avoid them. It is at those moments of greatest failure, sorrow and loss that we most feel alone and wonder about the apparent absence of God. It is during those times that God is nearest if we but look up and reach out our hand and ask for the safety and comfort of a loving and caring God.

THE STORM

GOD CARES

*He could see that they were worn out with rowing
since the wind was against them.* —MARK 6:48

1. Jesus Saw—At the breaking of dawn Jesus came to the disciples. Those in the boat had battled the storm all night. The sail had been lowered but the wind pushed the boat toward dangerous shores, and those in the boat couldn't know if they were to be dashed against rocks. So, they fought the storm, rowing to stay away from danger, bailing to keep the boat from sinking. As the sun was about to break above the horizon, there was enough light to see Him near to them, but not enough light yet to recognize Him. He was there for them. He saw and knew their need of Him. They were at their limits of endurance from the effort. That was when Jesus appeared.

2. Francis Saw—Whether Francis was in Gubbio at the time or came to Gubbio to aid the town is not known. What is told is that Francis had compassion on the people of Gubbio and decided to go out to the wolf even though the citizens advised against it. He took no weapon. He went defenseless other than the protection of the sign of the most holy cross, placing all his confidence in his God. What could Francis offer the town as protection against the wolf? Certainly, he did not go out with the intention of destroying the wolf. So what was Francis' goal? What could he accomplish? At such times, against all odds, is when we are most inclined to give in. It is at such times when God reveals Himself. It is not God's will that we break under strain of worry and fear, but it is His desire that we learn our absolute need of Him.

3. God Cares—It is the quality of the hero that God seeks in us. It is not a broken and defeated person that God wants of us. It is when the father sees his child persist against the odds that brings him delight and makes his heart proud with deserving pride. It is not in victory but in effort that the prize is won. We face life as it comes, knowing full well that God cares, that He sees our need. Through our prayer, His grace is enough for us to be God's hero every day.

THE STORM

No Fear

Courage! It is I! Do not be afraid. —Matt 14:27

1. They Didn't Expect Jesus—Those in the boat saw Him walking on the water but thought it a spirit and were terrified and yelled out in fear. A spirit would be a manifestation of evil, and by now they were broken men and expected the worst. They didn't expect Jesus. Jesus calmed them and told them that it was He. He was coming; they were not to be afraid. Their experience of Jesus was not yet enough to trust in Him without His presence. They were yet to learn to trust always and to have "No Fear" for He is always near.

2. The Wolf Didn't Expect Francis—It is likely others had come into the forest to kill the wolf, and the wolf may have been old and injured. Regardless, the wolf viewed Francis as an enemy, one to be feared, and one to be killed. The wolf charged to attack Francis. His animal instincts were aroused to kill or be killed. He took the initiative and in his fear of man sought to destroy Francis. As the wolf came close, Francis blessed the wolf with the sign of the holy cross and called him to himself saying, *"Come here, Brother Wolf, do not be afraid. I command you in the name of Jesus to do no harm."* The wolf came and lay at Francis' feet.

3. Do I Expect Him?—It is human nature that if I expect nothing, nothing will probably happen. However, if we expect a manifestation of God in a place, or an event, or in a person, usually we find that manifestation and are pleasantly surprised. The real surprise would be if we were not to find a manifestation of God, for the Creator has left His sign on all that He created and on every creature. We are to expect the manifestation of God in all experiences of life. All of the blessings and beauty in life as well as all of the suffering and losses, even the approach of death, should awaken to us great possibilities and a greater awareness of God.

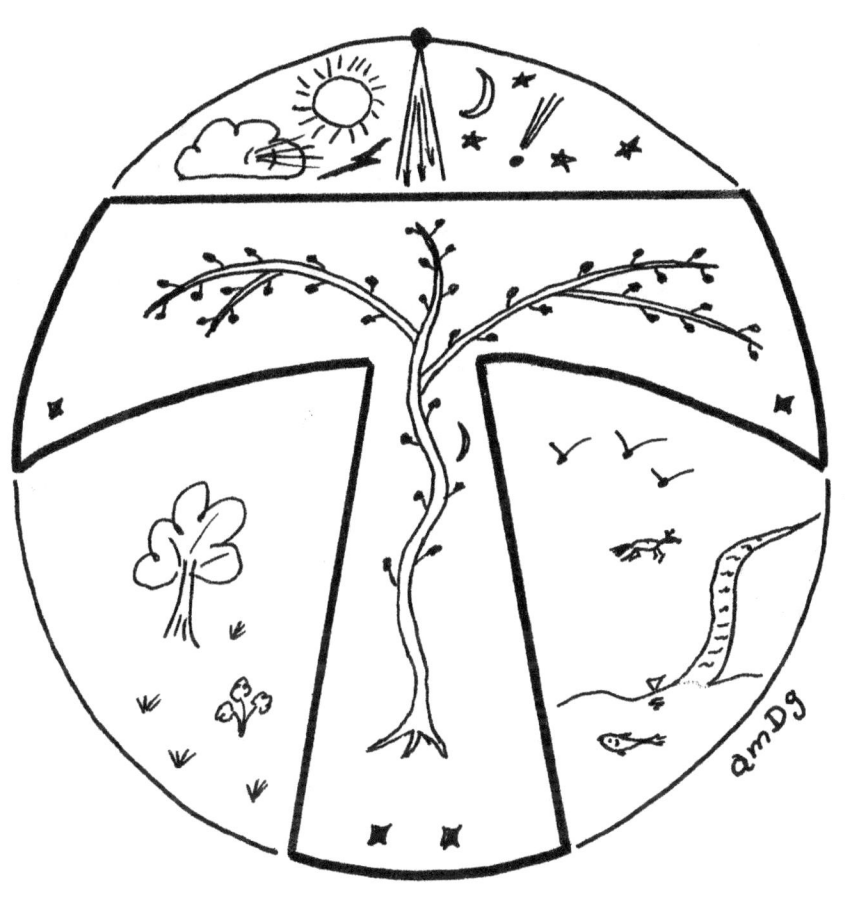

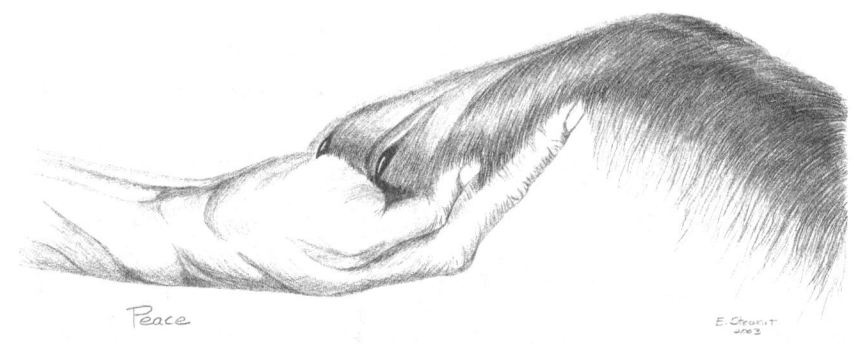

Peace by Esther Stewart

THE STORM

Keep Our Eyes on Jesus

Jesus put out His hand at once and held him. —MATT 14:31

1. Jesus Reached Out to Peter—There is something about Peter that we all embrace. Maybe it is his willingness and ability to cast all to the wind once he was convinced of a possibility. Jesus had appeared and hailed them. Peter then asked Jesus to call to Him and Jesus said, *"Come."* Peter at once got out of the boat and did the impossible, as Jesus said. All was wonderful, then came the harsh reality. The wind was throwing water in his face, and the waves were now breaking over his feet and legs. He took his eyes off of Jesus and immediately went down. And Jesus reached out and held him safe.

2. Francis Reached Out to the Wolf—Francis talked to the wolf, called him Brother, and said to him, *"You have done much harm and the town is now your enemy, but I, Brother Wolf, want to make peace between you and these people."* Saint Francis asked the wolf to promise to do no more harm to the town and, as a sign of the promise, Francis reached out his right hand and the wolf lifted his right paw and placed it on the outstretched hand of Francis, giving the only sign of acceptance that a wolf could make.

3. Jesus' Hand Is Always Extended to Us—Our failures, our losses, are just reminders along the way to keep our eye on Jesus and, when our eye drifts away and we begin to sink, to reach out our hand to the already outstretched hand of Jesus. It is when we think we are strong that we sink, and when we acknowledge our weaknesses that we achieve the unexpected. It is for me to remember, through prayer and humility, that I am as precious to Jesus as Peter was. He calls to me to do the remarkable and He is there to rescue me when I fail.

THE STORM

THEY WERE AMAZED

Truly, you are the Son of God. —MATT 14:33

1. The Disciples Were Amazed—Jesus and Peter got into the boat and the wind stopped. The disciples on the boat were overwhelmed with the display and presence of supernatural power among them, and they bowed down to Jesus and proclaimed Him the Son of God. That He or anyone else walked on water did not matter nor that He could stop the wind from blowing. Those signs themselves were not important to Jesus. What mattered is that those in the boat came to the conclusion on their own that Jesus was not simply a man or even a prophet but was, in fact, the Son of God. All of His works were merely signposts of the truth. What He did was not as important as who He was.

2. The People Were Amazed—Francis, with the wolf at his side and the followers maybe some steps behind, entered Gubbio and the crowded piazza. When the people were assembled, Francis, filled with the presence of God, preached to the people. Surely, he used the example of the wolf to remind the people to fear the evil that can devour the soul rather than that which can only kill the body. Brother Wolf once more placed his paw in the hand of Francis as a promise to the people to do them no harm, and the people promised to give the wolf what he needed every day. The people rejoiced for the devotion of the saint and the miracle of brotherly love and compassion that defeated fear and violence.

3. My Amazement—Is the wonder of Jesus not to be experienced in our time? Is the miracle of the wolf of Gubbio never to be repeated? Can fear be vanquished by faith? Can I call those that oppose me and who I may fear my brother rather than my enemy? Is Jesus to me what He was to those in the boat? Can I be like Saint Francis, an instrument of peace to the world? Only the conviction of God as the sustaining energy and life-giving presence in my life enables me to trust my life entirely and without reservation to the divine power of Jesus Christ. Only then is all possible.

SONS OF GOD

*Think of the love that the Father has lavished on us
by letting us be called God's children.* —1 John 3:1

1. Already the Children of God—Being a child of God is not something that
   we choose ourself and it is not to be earned on our own. It simply is. It is
   a condition of life, of being born human. It cannot be denied any more
   than we can deny the air that we breathe, and it is an essential element in
   which we live. As the children of God, we share divine life with Jesus, God
   become man, through the will of the Spirit. As a father loves his children
   so the perfect God perfectly loves us.

2. Simple, Humble and Pure—In the *Later Admonition and Exhortation to
   the Brothers and Sisters of Penance*, later known as the Order of Franciscans
   Secular, Francis warned against living wisely and prudently as the world
   would have us, but rather to be simple, humble and pure as God would
   have us as His children. Francis was wisely directing his followers to reflect
   good and, by so doing, to be known by the world by their likeness to the
   all-good God, our Father.

3. Our Responsibility—We are placed in the position of sons and daughters
   of God who know our Father. Ours is the honor of the Father's family.
   How do we show that honor? Am I merciful in my thoughts, generous in
   my giving, considerate in my actions, forgiving in my dealings with others, pure in my desires, humble in my successes, and simple in the way I
   choose to live? Those are the marks of a child of God. God has given His
   best to me as His heir. Do I give my best to others?

Sons of Zebedee by Kevin Novack

LANDOWNER AND LABORERS

GROW WHERE WE ARE PLANTED

He made an agreement with the workers. —MATT 20:2

1. God as Landowner—In the parable of the vineyard laborers, Jesus told of the landowner going out at daybreak to hire laborers for which they agreed to compensation for the day's work. The world is God's vineyard, and He chooses to use men and women as His laborers to bring other men and women to the full ripeness of His creation. God calls and expects all to labor in His vineyard in one fashion or another. He may call us at different times in our lives, some in our youth, some in the strength of our maturity, and others in the full experience of our life. God will call each of us at one time or another, or possibly at multiple times as His desire and our abilities ripen like fruit to be harvested and consumed to give sustenance to others. Our work will be shown to us; we are but to tend to the crops so that they may grow where God plants and bear the bounty of creation for all.

2. Francis as Vineyard Laborer—Saint Francis responded to God's call after years of struggle, pain and wandering of body, mind and spirit. But as God planted, so Francis grew, being nurtured and tended daily by the Holy Spirit. Nor did Francis reap the blessings and joy of the Holy Spirit to himself. Rather, he poured himself out to others, nurturing, caring and forming his brothers and sisters. He taught all that joined him, men and women, young and old, rich and poor, to walk the sacred fields of simplicity and poverty with holy compassion for all, calling each of God's creation our brothers and sisters.

3. My Work to Do—In life, we are to grow where we are planted. Here and now, we may have already heard the Lord's call and, as such, we may already be in the field tending God's vineyard; or we may have heard the call and are on our way, or we may be waiting in the eleventh hour of our life. The time will come, in God's time, for surely we will be called to our work. God the Father is a gracious and caring landowner, and He tends not only the land but the laborers as well. He will find us where we are in life at the time and place of His best knowing and will send each of us to where we are called to go. God has work for each of us to do for which we will be blessed and rewarded. My role is to show up in God's vineyard. Do I?

LANDOWNER AND LABORERS

God's Vision Is Beyond Ours

Why have you been standing here idle all day? —MATT 20:6

1. The Father Sees—In the parable, the landowner sees and cares that laborers have been idle all day while he has work to be done. So, he sends them into the field even though it is near the end of the day. God the Father sees and knows and cares about each of us and about the dignity that we can bring, not only to ourselves, but also the good that we bring to others by doing His work. So the Father calls to us where we are and dignifies us to be His hands in the fields with our brothers and sisters.

2. Francis' Vision—When there were but eight brothers, Francis wished that God would show him the course of his life and the future of the small brotherhood. Withdrawn to a place of prayer, gradually tremendous joy and sweetness of spirit came upon him. He returned to the brothers with joy, telling them that the Lord had shown him that God will make the few brothers grow into a great multitude, spreading them to the ends of the earth, and a great wave of people would come to them. Then Francis sent them in pairs through different parts of the world, announcing peace to all people. They were to be patient in trials with confidence that the Lord would fulfill His plans, to respond humbly to those that questioned them, to bless those that rejected them, and to thank those that harmed them. Francis embraced them and spoke sweetly to each, telling them to cast their care upon the Lord and He will sustain them.

3. The Vision of Myself—What vision of myself do I wish to become? Am I content to stand idle in God's workplace, or am I attentive to God's invitation to go into His vineyard? We are children of God, and the Father knows that the child is happy when he or she is engaged with doing, not simply being. In God's creation, it is not that many are called, but that all are called to be the best version of themselves. All I need do is be attentive to the call and to say "yes," trusting in the Holy Spirit to give me all that I need to fulfill the day and receive joy and grace at day's end.

LANDOWNER AND LABORERS

JOY

My friend, I am not being unjust to you. —MATT 20:13

1. **God's Joy in Our Work**—In the parable by Jesus, the landowner negotiated with the first group of morning laborers for a fair wage to which they agreed. When the landowner returned to the marketplace throughout the day, he could have negotiated with each as to the day's wages but apparently did not. Rather, at the end of the day he chose to pay them all the same as that pay negotiated with the first group, even though some had worked a whole day, others less and some only an hour or so. Jesus did not explain why the landowner did this nor does He justify the landowner's action. Jesus simply said that the landowner had a right to do as he wanted and that he was generous. The landowner was pleased with the work of all the laborers, and it gave him joy to reward each, in some cases even beyond what was fair.

2. **Franciscan Joy**—As the early brotherhood grew, they found joy in coming together. They regarded themselves as useless servants of God. Saint Francis and the brothers felt great gladness and exquisite joy whenever someone, led by the Holy Spirit, joined the brotherhood. Whether noble or peasant, rich or poor, wise or illiterate, cleric or lay, nothing would stand in the way of God building up his laborers to send into the world. The brothers were a great wonder to the world and an example of humility, challenging the world to a life of God's joy.

3. **My Work Is My Joy**—To look for reward and recognition is human. But in doing God's work it is better to leave it to God for the reward. To bargain with God may mean that we get what we bargained for but not what He has to give us. Working for the Lord transforms us. It is to enter into the joy of God and it brings the joy of living. Work for God, work for joy, for the reward is out of this world.

Tau drawn by Saint Francis on the wall of the Chapel
of Mary Magdalene at Fonte Colombo

WITNESS TO JESUS

Yes, I have seen and I am the witness that
He is the chosen one of God. —JOHN 1:34

1. John the Baptist as Witness—John was sent as the herald of Jesus the
    Christ to the Jewish people. For more than 2000 years, from the disciples
    and apostles to Peter and Paul, through the saints and all the holy men
    and women of God, we have witnesses to Jesus Christ, the Son of God.

2. Francis as Witness—Saint Francis heard Pope Innocent III at the open-
    ing of the 4th Lateran Council preach on Ezekiel 9:4 where the people of
    God were marked with the sign of tau on their foreheads—a sign that they
    belonged to God. To Francis that was a sign of renewal and of embrace
    of the cross of Jesus. Thereafter, Francis signed his name with tau, and
    he left record of that on the parchment given to Brother Leo and on the
    wall of the chapel at Fonte Colombo. Francis, in a sackcloth tunic with
    rope around his waist and a tau chalked on front and back, made his way
    as the herald of the Great King. Like John the Baptist, Francis was wit-
    ness to Jesus Christ, the Son of God, and also a herald to our salvation
    through the cross.

3. Our Witness—Many today want signs from God, specific actions and
    miracles. We want wars stopped, the sick healed, the starving fed. But
    our witness, if we are to truly witness to Jesus, shall be in the little signs:
    prayer, humility, simplicity, purity, trust in God, by our faithfulness not by
    our successes. Our witness is founded on the witness of others; we stand
    on the shoulders of those who have gone before us. And each shall find
    something new in Him. So shall I, for His grace and His gifts are never
    exhausted. I may not be called to witness as John and Francis, but I am
    called. What symbol of belonging to God shall I leave?

TRUST

Take nothing for the journey: neither staff, nor
haversack, nor bread, nor money; and let none
of you take a spare tunic. —LUKE 9:3

1. Mission of the Twelve—The twelve apostles, having been with Jesus awhile,
   had heard Him preach the Good News and had seen Him perform cures.
   But hearing and seeing are one thing, understanding is another. They, as
   yet, did not understand the message of Jesus. Jesus came to proclaim to all,
   once and for all, the Kingdom of God on earth. For the apostles to begin
   to understand, they had to do as Jesus did; they had to preach the Good
   News and to heal the infirmed. Surely Jesus gave them instructions and
   assured them of the power and authority that He gave them. But Jesus
   knew that the spirit must be strengthened by trust. It is only through trust
   that they could confidently proclaim the Kingdom of God, only through
   trust that they could heal. In taking nothing for the journey the apostles
   would learn trust in Him and begin their journey of believing in Him who
   sent them. The true mission of the twelve was to personally witness to
   the power of trust in God; preaching and healing were simply the means.

2. Mission of Saint Francis—Hearing the gospel of Luke, Francis set his life's
   mission to following the words of Jesus. In so doing, Francis would take
   nothing for the journey—no bread, no money and no spare tunic. Nor
   would he be outdone in his zeal for the word of the gospel. Once when
   coming upon a poor man who had a cloak that was more miserable than
   his own, Francis exchanged cloaks with him. To his followers Francis
   said that he must "return" his cloak to the poor man to whom it belongs
   because it was only on "loan" to him until he came upon someone poorer
   than he. In completely trusting God, Francis renounced ownership and
   sought only to give, never to receive.

3. Mission of Doing—In striving to learn, it is said, "To hear is to forget, to see
   is to remember, to do is to understand." It was not enough for the apostles to
   hear the words of Jesus or to see his deeds. It was not enough for Francis
   to hear the Good News. For each it was in the doing that they understood
   their life's mission, in doing that they learned trust in God, in doing that
   they possessed the Kingdom of God.

ETERNAL LIFE

Go and sell everything that you own and give the money to
the poor, and you will have treasure in heaven. —MARK 10:21

1. Nothing—The rich, young man asked Jesus what was necessary to inherit
   eternal life. He already had much in this life, but he wanted more: He
   wanted eternal life, he wanted everything. Jesus, loving him, said that to have
   everything he must give up all that he had and follow him. Incomprehensible
   to the young man that to have the best was to relinquish that which he
   possessed, he went away sad.

2. Everything—Francis of Assisi, the son of a wealthy merchant, the son of a
   loving, caring mother, the troubadour with his friends, the knight in armor
   on a fine warhorse, the poet, the lover, had all that the world declares of
   value: wealth, comfort, prestige, health and love. In his *Testament*, Francis
   says that he left the world. In his conversion to Christ, rather than being
   flung to the ground from his horse by Christ as was Saint Paul, Saint
   Francis chose to cast himself to the ground from his high horse for Jesus.
   His father had called him a thief, the military called him a coward, and to
   the town he was a fool. Through his love of God, in his youthful despair
   he clung to hope; in doubt of his choices he embraced faith; every injury
   inflicted upon him brought pardon; darkness and hatred brought forth
   light and love; and where there could have been sadness was only joy.
   In giving himself to God, in emptying himself of the world, he gained
   everything—eternal life.

3. Expectations—For most of us we will be neither like the rich young man
   who, hearing God's call, that we depart in sadness, nor like Francis that
   we give up all in this life to do God's will. Likely, our path will be one of
   expectation in doing God's will as we hear it day-by-day: a life filled with
   giving, with pardoning and consoling, with seeking to understand, and
   to loving with passion. If so, our expectation can be that in dying we are
   born to eternal life.

EMMAUS

On the Way

Two of them were on their way to Emmaus,
seven miles from Jerusalem. —Luke 24:13

1. Given Up—Maybe Emmaus was their home. They had left all of that behind to follow Jesus. Maybe they had been with Jesus when He made His entry into Jerusalem only a week earlier. They had expectations of greatness, of the coming of the messiah. Jesus would lead the cause of the nation and restore glory and power to Israel. Now Jesus was dead. So many of their prophets of old had died such as this, and dead men don't lead. They were dejected and their cause had ended. It was over. They were going home. Home to what? They walked along empty, drained of all that they wanted, all that they believed in, all that could be hoped for.

2. Fear—The love of Lady Poverty was Francis' dream. That was how he knew to follow Jesus. To live the gospel message was his all. But would his brothers have the same dream? Could they embrace poverty and find the same love that he found? To be poor meant hardship. It meant working each day, and when there is no work or no time for work, to beg for food and to eat what was given. It meant uncertainty of traveling on foot, sometimes in the rain and cold, with no hope of a warm, dry resting place at the end. It meant being rejected by their loved ones and being called a fool by many. Would the hardship, the doubt, be too much for them? Would they leave him and return to their home? But beyond fear of losing his brothers, losing those that he loved, was a greater fear. He feared that having found the pearl of great price, the way would become too difficult for him, that he would turn away from Lady Poverty and turn back home to the life that he had left behind.

3. Spiritual Darkness—The disciples on the way to Emmaus were suffering the darkness of the soul. They had lost all hope of God. Worse, they had lost hope in themselves. The dark days of the soul come to all; whether it be by actual loss or just the fear of the loss, the darkness is real and frightening. During that time of darkness we must cling to hope, to have patience with God. He will not leave the faithful and loving soul without comfort. Remember the good, for the goodness of God is in the darkness as well as the light. Be patient with God, and with yourself, and with others.

JESUS DREW NEAR

Jesus, himself came up and walked by their side. —LUKE 24:15

1. Spiritual Expectations—It is easy to picture the two disciples walking along the road with their heads hung down, lost in thought, only occasionally engaging the other with some remembrance or question. As Jesus drew alongside and eventually engaged them with a gentle, unassuming manner, they hardly noticed or even looked into His face. They were lost in their own thoughts of what should have happened, their expectations of God. Jesus was to restore Israel. It was not possible to see another reality. Their expectations of God blinded them to the reality of the Son of Man that they thought that they knew, but they hadn't. That reality was yet to be learned.

2. Finding God—We can imagine Francis of Assisi pondering the question, "Where is God?" Was He in the churches that he repaired, or the cities that he visited, or in the cave, or on the road along the way, or only in the Eucharist? Francis' experience in the cave had assured him that Jesus was with him and dwelt inside of him, that God Himself was within his heart, and further, that God was in the heart of all. For Francis that expectation of the presence of God was to be found in the first letter of John the Apostle, *"God is love and anyone who lives in love lives in God, and God lives in him."* Francis carried love with him on the road, or in a church, or in a cave, or in receiving Eucharist, and in so doing he found God in everything and everyone all along the way.

3. Find What You Bring—What are my expectations for finding God? Is my purpose to look for Him in all of the "right" places, in churches, in creation, in experiences and miracles, in the Eucharist? If so, I, too, may miss God along the way, for my expectation of God may not be God's reality. Or like Francis, do I find God wherever I am because I bring love with me wherever I am? Love is the eternal gift of God because He first loved us and we have but to love in return to find God. To look for God is to look for love. To find love is to bring love. To bring love is to find God. Do I?

EMMAUS

JESUS NOT RECOGNIZED

Something prevented them from recognizing Him. —LUKE 24:16

1. Spiritual Blindness—The senses of the disciples were blinded to the physical presence of Jesus. Possibly His spirituality so powerfully manifested itself that His physical being was obscured much as flame can conceal that which is being burned. Whatever the reason, Jesus was so changed that He was not recognized. Normally, physical change is slow and can barely be detected day after day. But Jesus' change was radical, as in the blinking of an eye. The disciples needed to see Him in a different light, to see Him in the light of His spiritual life.

2. Spiritual Transformation—From the beginning of his conversion as he walked away from his father and the bishop to his death on the ground at the Portiuncula, Francis' spirit was transformed a bit at a time. With each experience, from embracing the leper, petitioning the pope, befriending the sultan, welcoming Clare to the brotherhood, and to the terror of his eye disease, Francis moved spiritually as God willed, a bit at a time. Where did Francis find the strength for such continuous, blessed transformation? Surely it was in Francis' prayer. Francis, too, like Jesus, would climb the mountain and give himself up in prayer that he could be spiritually changed, bit by bit, into the reality that God had for him. For it was no longer the dream of Francis that he lived for, but the reality of God's dream for him that he longed for, prayed for. The spiritual transformation for Francis was slow and grew with each prayer along the spiritual way.

3. Little by Little—The disciples of Jesus had to grow spiritually to know the real Jesus, not the Jesus that they expected. Francis, to achieve the dream that God had for him, had to grow spiritually little by little. If we but persist in faith and prayer, that spiritual growth will manifest itself and we will be a light to the world. Love Jesus as did the disciples on the road to Emmaus, as Francis did, and we, too, will be spiritually transformed before the world.

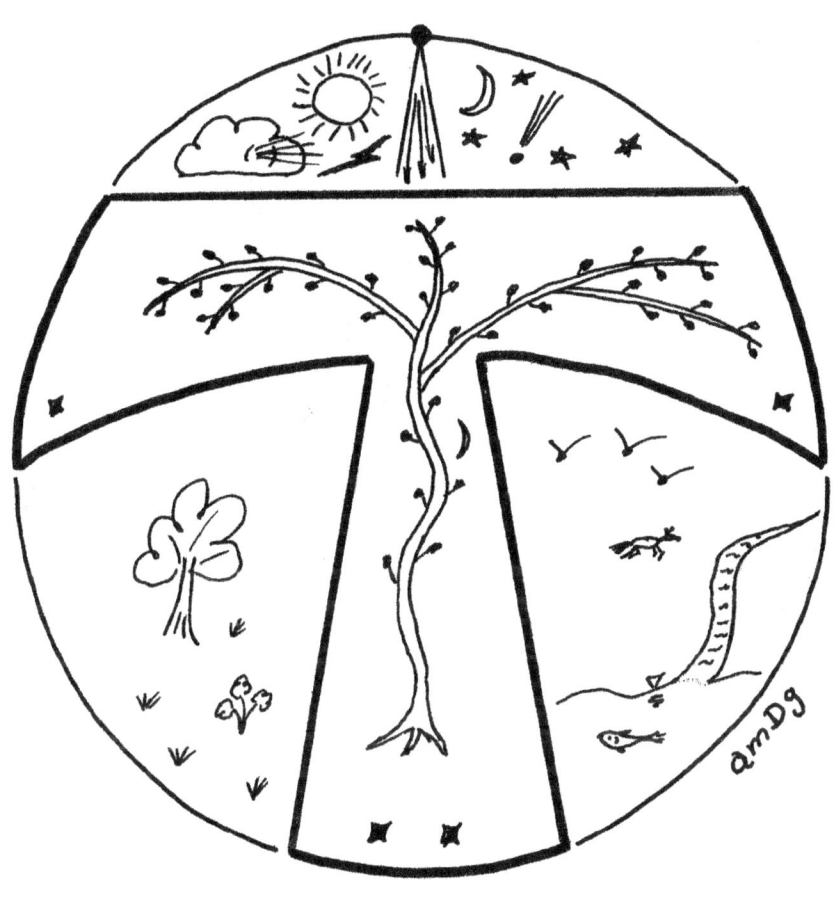

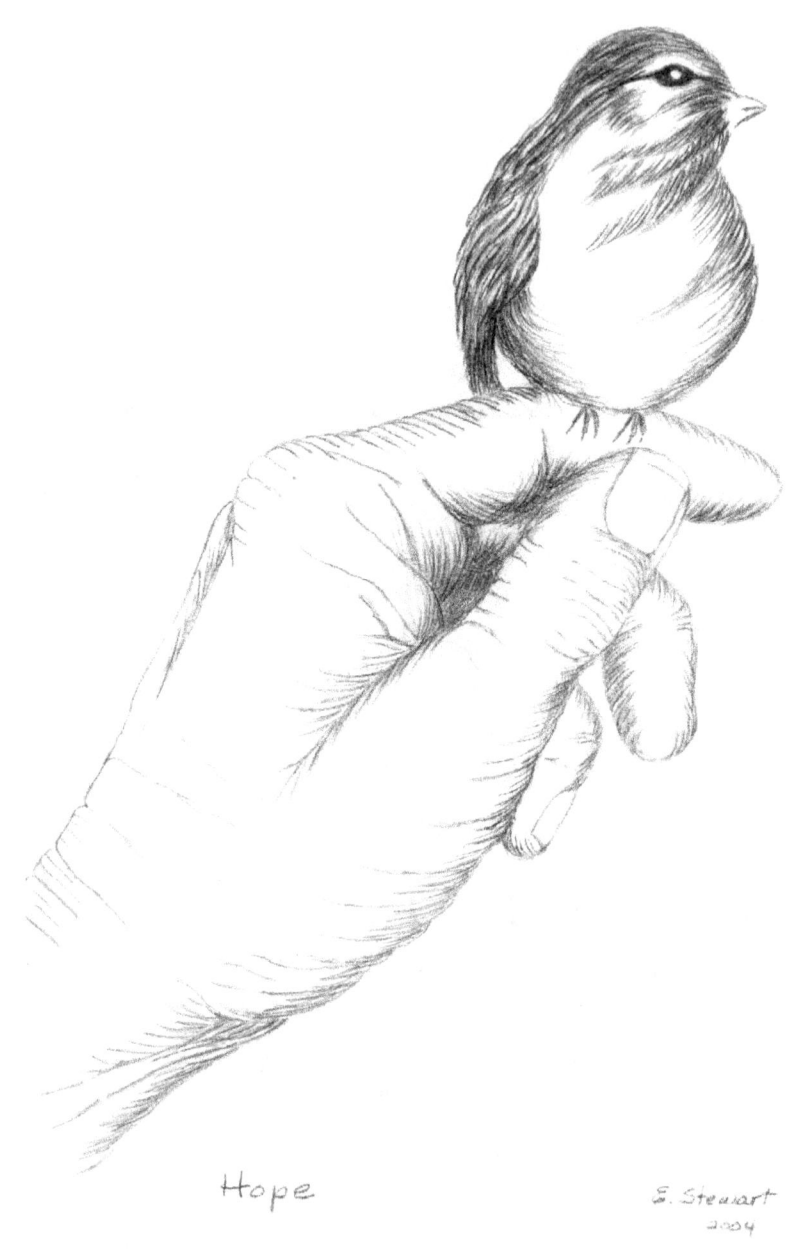

Hope

E. Stewart
2004

Hope by Esther Stewart

84

EMMAUS

THEY SHOULD HAVE KNOWN

Then He said to them, "You foolish men." —LUKE 24:25

1. Slow to Believe—The disciples should have known that Jesus would rise. The prophets had foretold the message; the women at the tomb told them that angels declared that He was alive. Jesus himself told them that He was to be crucified and rise in three days. Foolish men indeed! What prevented them from accepting that which was plainly before them? They had blinded themselves with what they believe should be. Their sorrow was all their own making. They could have chosen to rejoice and should have.

2. From Gospel to Life—Francis was not content to hear the gospel. He consumed the gospel until it was of him, alive, and released to the world with every breath, every word, every look, nod and touch. Since Jesus was not only within him but of him, he could see the Creator in all creation. Jesus had said that His Father cared for all, even the flowers in the field and the birds in the air. If so, then Francis must tell even the birds about Jesus and how the Father cares for them. Francis loved most tenderly the larks that sang for joy and soared in freedom. Maybe Francis saw in the larks the resurrected Jesus soaring on wings of joy and freedom for all to see and to remember His words that we, too, are to soar like larks for all to see and know the promises of Jesus and the loving care of the Father.

3. Dare to Believe—The prophets and scripture told of Jesus; the disciples of Jesus told us who He was and what He did; our parents and Church family teach us to believe and listen to the word of God. All of the promises of God are there before us if we dare to believe. I cannot escape the presence of God; He will make Himself known to me if I but dare to be open to all that is before me. Even the lark is a reminder of the resurrection of Jesus and all that is promised to us. I am ready, Lord, I am ready.

EMMAUS

JESUS THE CHRIST SUFFERED

*Was it not ordained that the Christ should suffer
and so enter into His glory?* —LUKE 24:26

1. Suffering as Part of the Whole—The disciples were lost at the death of Jesus. The living Jesus was their entire hope, not only for the nation but more importantly for each of them individually. Now He was dead and all of their hopes and dreams had died with Him. Life had been full of meaning only a few days ago and now it was gone. They should have known better. Suffering and death are part of the whole of life, and so it was with Jesus. But death is not the end, nor is suffering unto itself the purpose of life. So for Jesus, suffering and death were part of the whole. If the disciples had accepted the suffering and death of Jesus, they could have accepted His resurrection and glory. His resurrection was fulfillment of His promise of the Kingdom of God and His righteousness.

2. Alone with the Lepers—Before Francis had brothers, he was alone in his care for the lepers in the swampy plains below Assisi. Although consoled in the good that he did for the lepers, surely there would have been times when he wondered if anyone other than the lepers knew or cared for what he did. If to be merciful meant to have mercy shown to him, where was that mercy? If to have love for the lepers, where was the love that he needed? Francis learned and understood that real love was hard and difficult to sustain. Real love was not all sweetness and comforting feelings deep inside. Nor would love always be returned, regardless of how one loved.

3. Mystery of Suffering—There is a capacity for suffering that is both thrust upon us to be either accepted or to rebel against, but the suffering remains. Suffering is, at best, a mystery of this life. We may well ask the purpose of suffering and not find an answer that can be accepted or gives us comfort. Maybe, like the saints, the nearer we get to God through association with His son, Jesus, the greater our capacity and acceptance of suffering. If Jesus had escaped suffering and death, He would not have had resurrection. He would not have it so, nor should we.

EMMAUS

Stay with Us

When they drew near to Emmaus, He made as if to go on,
but they pressed Him to stay with them. —Luke 24:28

1. Heaven's Work—Jesus had renewed their spirits. They were no longer
    without hope but were enlightened and of fresh enthusiasm. As if to cel-
    ebrate but certainly to hear more from the stranger, they entreated Him to
    stay the evening with them. They owed much to Him, and a meal together
    would further cement the bond that had so quickly formed. They would
    at least thank Him with a meal, and maybe He had more to tell of Jesus
    and His resurrection. So, Jesus entered the house and at their bidding sat
    at table with them. How pleased they were with their good fortune, but
    how little they knew then that Jesus had submitted Himself into their
    hands. Our work is best done when it is Heaven's work.

2. The Gospel's Work—If Francis was a fool to others, it was because he was
    first God's fool to the gospel. What he heard, he believed. If Jesus meant
    other interpretations of His word, that was not for Francis. If Jesus had
    no place to lay His head, then neither would Francis. If to be poor in spirit
    was to be blessed, then he would be the poorest. If the road of life was
    narrow and difficult, then that was the path that he chose. To follow the
    gospel was the work of a lifetime for Francis. The road for him and his
    brothers wasn't the easy road but it would be Heaven's road, and Francis
    was to do Heaven's work.

3. My Work—What is my work in this life? What is the road that I have
    chosen? Who is on that road with me? Whether I invite Jesus or not, He
    is there with me. If I but open my heart's eyes, I will see Him. Jesus, who
    would have me as a companion, is already with me. Jesus, who I would
    possess is in my heart now. Jesus was on the road to Emmaus and Jesus
    was on the roads of Umbria with Francis, and Clare, and the brothers
    and sisters. If I do my work as Jesus calls to me, I will see Him with every
    step that I take.

EMMAUS

In the Breaking of the Bread

While He was with them at table, He took the
bread and said the blessing, then He broke it
and handed it to them. —Luke 24:30

1. Their Eyes Were Opened—The disciples had seen Jesus say the blessing, break the bread, and give it out before. Maybe they had been with Him when He fed the 5,000, or had been at table with Him at other times. No one could bless bread as He did. It was then that they knew Him. They were alive again. All was well. How did they react? Did they laugh with joy as they realized their foolishness? Surely the shock was too much other than possibly to cry out, *"My Lord."* Then in the silence, the awe of the moment, now what? To reach out, to embrace Him, but He vanished from them. All was done. They had seen, they knew, they believed. They hurried back to Jerusalem with a light for all generations to see, to know, to believe in Jesus the Christ.

2. Transformed into Christ—Saint Francis and the little brothers were transformed men. Saint Clare and the little sisters were transformed women. It was transformed men and transformed women who would transform the world, who would rebuild the Church. The bread and wine transformed into Christ can transform people into Christ if they are but willing to be transformed. Jesus can then transform people so that others can see Jesus in them and be transformed themselves. That was a dream of Francis and Clare, to be so transformed into Jesus that they would be Eucharist for others, and the transformation would go on one to another over the ages. So it has been, from Emmaus to Assisi to our time, holy men and women transformed by the Eucharist and into the Eucharist have hurried to us so that we may in turn be transformed and that Jesus may be seen by our blessed presence.

3. My Transformation—We know Him in the breaking of the bread. Parent has called to child in generation upon generation. The Church continues its witness to Jesus the Christ and continues its transforming power to the world. What would the Church be without Eucharist? What would the world be without the Church? More importantly, what am I with the Eucharist and how am I the image of Christ to others? I am to be the bread and the wine blessed and broken to be given to others. Am I?

HERALDS OF JESUS

Philip said to Jesus, "Lord, show us the Father,
that is all we need." —John 14:8

1. Jesus Pointed to the Father—In response to Philip, Jesus said that the words that He spoke did not come from Him but from the Father. In that act, Jesus pointed to the Father, not to Himself. All of Jesus' life, from His birth to His death, pointed to His oneness with God the Father. In fact, Jesus had been showing them the Father all along. Not only the words but the works of Jesus are the works of the Father. As Jesus loved them, so the Father loved them. As they love Him, so, too, they love the Father.

2. Francis Pointed to the King—As John the Baptist had been the herald of Jesus in life, so Francis was the herald of the triumphant King. As John was dressed, so Francis dressed in his tattered tunic with the sign of tau chalked on it and a rope about his waist. As he walked the roads and as he entered the towns, he cried out to all in a loud, proud voice, "*I am the herald of the King of Kings.*" His whole being, his whole life pointed to none other than his King, the sole possessor of his body, mind and spirit. There was no distraction, there was no misdirection, there was no other purpose for Francis. All creation pointed to Jesus, the King of Kings, and he would not be outdone, not even by Brother Sun or Sister Moon.

3. The Communion of Saints Points to Jesus—From Saint Peter and Saint Paul and the apostles down through the ages, all of the saints pointed to Jesus in word and action. For many of us, those before us, our parents and grandparents, our friends and life's companions have pointed to Jesus for us. Without others showing us the way, we may have groped and stumbled, missing the mark in life. So, as those before us, we, too, are called like John the Baptist, like Francis and Clare, like the entire Communion of Saints to point to Jesus, to be heralds to the King of Kings.

Martha and Mary by Kevin Novack

MARTHA AND MARY

MARTHA'S SERVICE

Lord, do you not care that my sister is leaving me to do the serving all by myself? Please tell her to help me. —LUKE 10:40

1. Martha's Service to Jesus—Martha, her sister Mary, and their brother Lazarus were close and loving friends of Jesus, as we know from several accounts in the gospels. In this account, Jesus was welcomed into Martha's house where she proceeded to prepare to serve Jesus. However, Mary sat at Jesus' feet and listened to Him speak. This story is often used to relate those that choose to live a life of service and those that choose a contemplative life of prayer. Jesus' answer to Martha that Mary has chosen the better part would seem to indicate that the withdrawal from life's responsibilities is the better part. However, it equally shows the deep humanity of Jesus in that the attention and affection of loved ones is far greater and desired than sustenance by "bread alone." Jesus' response to Mary is that only one thing is necessary, and that one thing is the Word of God.

2. Francis' Service to God—At one point in his life, Francis questioned whether he should continue his life as an itinerant preacher or if he should retire to a quiet life of prayer and contemplation. Francis sent Brother Masseo to Clare and to Brother Sylvester to ask their advice. Clare and Brother Sylvester prayed for guidance from God. Both heard in their hearts that Francis was not called into this life for his own benefit, but that he was called to serve the needs of many and to reap a harvest of souls for God.

3. My Service to God and Mankind—The duty and the reward of the God-centered life is in the living of it. The question is not whether we are to live a life of service or a life of prayer, but how we are to live a life of service and prayer. It is not easy for us to decide how we are to best serve God in this life. Like Francis, we, too, need our Brother Masseo, our Sister Clare, and our Brother Sylvester to support, encourage and affirm us in our chosen way. Nor are we called to be either Martha or Mary—for only one thing is necessary, and that is to be the Word of God in both service and prayer to one another.

MARTHA AND MARY

PRIORITY

Jesus replied, "Man does not live on bread alone." —LUKE 4:4

1. Jesus' Priority—At the end of 40 days in the wilderness of fasting and prayer, Jesus was hungry. The devil tempted Jesus to turn a rock into bread, but Jesus resisted. His answer is inspirational. There is dignity in who we are that goes beyond what we do. Jesus' body was a temple of God and had a purpose far beyond the sustenance of human life. In Jesus' declaration is the utterance of all that Jesus is. His living and dying would be the redemption of the world and all people for all time from the power of evil and deliverance to the abundance of an all-good God.

2. Francis' and Clare's Priority—"For the love of my Lord and Savior Jesus Christ" was the guiding light and beacon of hope in the wilderness of a dark world calling all to a loving God that cares and sustains all creatures. Francis was in love with the crucified Jesus. Jesus was real; He lived and died to show us the love that His Father has for all of His children. Clare saw that Francis was in love with the Lord and that love of God would never change; it was unconditional. It made no difference to Francis or Clare what activity they embarked on or what challenge they faced, or how they served others. They always kept God at the center of their being and their heart's one desire. Truly, Francis and Clare understood and embraced a life in God and with God that far surpassed life alone.

3. My Priority—With God at the center of our lives, all else takes its rightful place. The mind and body are in step with the soul that is in harmony with God. Our priority is God's priority, we love what God loves, we will what God wills, and we will do in this life what God would have us do. What are my priorities? Is God the center of the purpose of all that I am? If so, Jesus will surely lead me down the right path, though I know nothing of it.

MARTHA AND MARY

VISION

Do not worry about your life . . . Set your hearts
on the kingdom of God. —MATT 6:25, 33

1. Jesus' View of Life—There can be, and often is, a gulf between the way
   that we see life and the way that Jesus would have us see it. Human existence requires that we tend to our earthly needs: to eat, to be clothed, to
   be sheltered and protected from the elements, to seek safety. Jesus does
   not ask us to abstain from the necessities of life. Jesus acknowledges those
   needs, whether they be the birds of the air or King Solomon. Rather, Jesus
   addresses our vision of life. Our life's vision is not to be set on the necessities and comforts of this life, but rather our vision is to set our hearts on
   what is truly worthy of us and fulfills our every desire and need.

2. Clare's View from San Damiano—Clare had relinquished her life of
   nobility for her view of creation in unity with Francis and being in oneness
   with the eternal Creator and all-good God. Her life with her sisters at
   San Damiano had set her free. She no longer needed to worry about what
   she was to wear, or how she was to speak, or the impression that she was
   to make on others as part of the nobility and landed gentry of Assisi. The
   world now presented itself without expectations or demands. Setting her
   vision on the Kingdom of God and not on the kingdoms of mankind had
   given her all things, not just some things. Through her God vision every
   flower in the garden was robed finer than a royal gown, every swallow in
   the sky soared with greater dominion over the land than the mightiest
   noble, and the breeze from Mount Subasio was sweeter than gold could
   purchase. She was rich beyond measure in the garden of San Damiano
   with her heart in the Kingdom of God.

3. My Life's View—My vision of life shows me something of myself. Certainly,
   I am not to live a carefree life without duty or purpose or obligation to
   myself and to others. But what of my higher duty, purpose and obligation
   to God? Is that not of greater essence and demand? I may not be called to
   live a monastic life, but I am called to a higher standard than that which
   the world has set. The abundance of God is before me if I can but set my
   vision day by day on His Kingdom and not the kingdom of man's making.

MARTHA AND MARY

TOUCHED BY ETERNITY

*Yes Lord, I believe that you are the Christ, the Son of God,
the one who was to come into the world.* —JOHN 11:27

1. Martha Is Touched by Jesus—Martha has known Jesus for some time. He is a dear friend of her and Mary and Lazarus who died and was buried four days ago. Jesus comes to Bethany and Martha goes to meet Him. In response to Martha, Jesus says that Lazarus will rise again and that He is the resurrection. Martha gives her affirmation of, *"Yes Lord, I believe."* With that there is a new relationship, Martha has a new purpose and direction in life. Jesus is no longer just a friend in this life; eternity has come to the relationship. Whoever believes in Jesus will never die. Until now Martha has been busy with life only in the present. Now, touched by Jesus, she will touch the lives of many, bringing all to eternity with her Lord.

2. Francis and Clare Were Touched—For much of their life Francis and Clare lived in a stormy present, clinging to a dream of the future, a dream founded in faith, nurtured by love, and sustained by a hope in the future. Little by little, day by day, person by person, they were touched by Jesus and grew into the fullness of being not just in the present but into eternity with God. It was only through their daily affirmation of *"Yes Lord, I believe"* that their dream of the lesser brothers and of the poor ladies became a reality. God, in touching Francis and Clare, touched the world.

3. I Am Touched—The reach of my dreams is to be more than of this present life. My dreams can and must reach into eternity for me and for all that I touch. The present is not the horizon, nor even the future. My life's horizon must be eternity. I was born into this life with God and I will leave this life with God. God holds me and infinity in the palm of His hand. What is my dream in this life? With what am I busy? Am I conscious of the touch of Jesus, the gentle whisper? With the acceptance and affirmation of the Eternal in my life will come fresh dreams, new awareness, clarity to my words, purpose to my deeds, and fulfillment for eternity. Yes Lord, I believe.

PRESENCE

As soon as Elizabeth heard Mary's greeting,
the child leapt in her womb. —LUKE 1:41

1. Mary to Elizabeth—Mary heard from the angel Gabriel that her cousin, Elizabeth, was six months pregnant. Elizabeth, being elderly, needed help, and Mary needed someone to help her comprehend the mystery of her pregnancy. Can we say who needed the other more? Was it the young, active Mary that was the most-needed responder, or was it the mature and wiser Elizabeth that gave the greater comfort? Surely it was both. Each was present to the other as was needed, and the babe John leapt for joy inside Elizabeth at the presence of Jesus in Mary's womb.

2. The Babe Jesus at Greccio—A few years before his death, Francis wanted to enact the birth of Jesus, and so the first Nativity celebration with a manger and animals took place in Greccio. A man of Greccio who came to the celebration saw a wondrous vision of a babe lying still in the manger and Francis awaken the babe from a deep sleep. The presence of the babe Jesus was awakened in the hearts of the people of Greccio, and forever after the hearts of many throughout the world have leapt for joy at the presence of the babe Jesus deep within our being.

3. A Time for Presence—For much of our culture and tradition Christmas is a time for presents, but much more important, it is a time for presence. During the season of Advent, the pace of life quickens for the Christian as we prepare for the celebration of Christmas with family and friends. Advent is a season to hasten, but to hasten as Mary hastened to be present to Elizabeth, as the shepherds hastened to the stable, as the people of Greccio hastened to prepare the stable and manger. In that haste we can hardly do better than to stop and be present to one another and let the joy of the babe Jesus leap in one another's hearts.

The Call to Follow by Kevin Novack

THE GOOD SHEPHERD

I am the good shepherd. —JOHN 10:11

1. Jesus Gathers His Flock—In this parable, Jesus calls Himself the good shepherd, one who knows His sheep and the sheep listen to His voice. He protects His sheep and will lay down His life for His sheep. Jesus said that the hired man does not know the sheep since they do not belong to him. When the wolf comes, the hired man abandons the sheep and runs away and the sheep are scattered. Not all who heard Jesus accepted His words or were willing to understand the message. This led to conflict, some refusing to listen any longer and others taking the image of a good shepherd to heart.

2. Francis as a Shepherd—Francis recognized that being a shepherd meant being at peace rather than in conflict—to be a peacemaker. Just as the sheep need green meadows and still waters to exist, so do all creatures need the essentials of life. Conflict in societies most often arises when there is a real or even a perceived unfair distribution of essentials. For Francis, the sharing of food, of clothing, of shelter and all good things, especially with those in most need, was a prerequisite for not only avoiding conflict but keeping peace. Time and time again, Francis lived the parable of a good shepherd. Never did one in need come to Francis and was turned away unaided, whether the poor beggar with a tattered cloak or a wretched leper. All were gathered into his loving embrace and care. Even the tale of the hungry wolf of Gubbio speaks of Francis' zeal to counter conflict with peace.

3. Brotherhood—To be a brother or a sister to one another requires more than words; actions are necessary if conflict is to be avoided. Do I recognize the needs of others and the often-unfair distribution of the essentials of life? Am I aware of the cause of conflicts in my life and do I work at being a peacemaker? What opportunities do I have for being a shepherd to others? Can I, like Francis, embrace the leper, clothe the beggar and reach out my hand in peace to the wolf?

SAINT THOMAS

SAINT THOMAS THE TWIN

Let us go too, and die with Him. —JOHN 11:16

1. A Great Lover—He is best known as "doubting Thomas," but the gospel records him as the twin, but twin to whom? Was he the natural twin to another, or possibly was he as much like Jesus in all his being as to be called His twin by the disciples? Possibly his love and his understanding of Jesus and His destiny may have been better understood by Thomas than the other disciples of Jesus. After Lazarus had died and Jesus said that He was going to Bethany near Jerusalem, the disciples warned Jesus that it wasn't long since the Jews wanted to stone Him there. Thomas said that they should go and die with Jesus. Only a great lover would be willing to join his friend in death. To be a great lover means to endure silently and to be courageous in waiting for the beloved, which Thomas would do later.

2. The Sign of a Lover—A common depiction of Saint Francis is his embracing the crucified Jesus on His cross. That Francis spiritually embraced the crucified Jesus is best known in his receipt of the wounds of Jesus at La Verna. Surely, it was only the love that Francis had for Jesus that gave him the strength and the courage to pray in his heart on La Verna as Saint Thomas did, "*Let me go too, and die with him.*" In the Franciscan coat of arms is the wounded arm of Jesus entwined with the stigmata arm of Francis over Christ's cross as a sign of the embrace of love between Jesus and Francis.

3. True Love—To love and to be loved is the best that we can strive for, hope for and achieve in this life. When we find evidence of such love, we mark it in history so that all can see, and remember, and know the truth of such love. Such is the story of Thomas and Francis and countless others. How shall they know us? How shall they know me? By our love.

SAINT THOMAS

Suffering Alone

Thomas was not with them when Jesus came. —John 20:24

1. Selfish Sorrow—After fleeing the garden with the others, Thomas knew that Jesus was condemned and crucified; that He was dead and buried. His grief and agony was intense. He lost the love of his life. Earlier he had been willing to die with Jesus, yet now he had abandoned Him, left Him to stand trial without as much of a word of testimony in His defense. What friend of Jesus was he? He was psychologically beaten, spiritually drained, emotionally destroyed. He withdrew from the world. What could the world offer? Worse, he abandoned his friends, his closest and dearest companions. They shared the same grief and they needed the strength of his character to help them understand. Thomas thought of no one but himself. What of Mary, Jesus' mother, did she not need Thomas to cling to in her sorrow?

2. Withdrawal to the Cave—Shortly after Francis' conversion and having embraced the leper, Bonaventure tells that Francis began to seek out solitary places that were favorable for grieving. Of what Francis grieved we can only imagine, but surely his thoughts were of Jesus Christ beaten and crucified. But was that grieving also at times of his personal loss? Would it not be natural to grieve the loss of his father? And what of his mother? Was she not also in grief at the loss of her son and the alienation of her husband? How much of Francis' withdrawal was a response to his call by God and how much possibly to misdirected personal grief and selfish self-pity? Could Francis have achieved all that he set for himself and still have left room for those that he loved and who loved him? Was it necessary for him to leave mother and father to follow God? Personal pursuits, no matter how good and noble, can be a painful burden to others.

3. The Test—Life will always present pain, sorrow and suffering. The test is the power of our love so as to set aside our personal grief to comfort others. Thomas loved Jesus powerfully; he could have used that power to aid his friends, and in that he failed and lost. Francis found the means to love Jesus powerfully in the cave of his grief, but at what cost to those who cherished him? How much room did Francis leave in the cave of his heart for his mother to enter, and for his father, too?

No More

*Unless I put my fingers in the holes the nails made and put
my hand into His side, I refuse to believe.* —John 20:25

1. We Have Seen the Lord—Thomas had abandoned his friends, but they remembered him in their joy. They sought out Thomas and told him the news. But Thomas could not believe. The pain was too great to be released based simply on words of others. Jesus had died. Dead men don't come back. They were wrong and maybe tricked by the Jews. He couldn't take the chance to be hurt again. He was resigned to the loss of his dear friend and couldn't suffer that disappointment again. He demanded proof that was impossible to deliver. But, oh, the looks on their faces told the story. Yes, Thomas, you will see and you will believe. It will be wonderful to be there.

2. On Mount Subasio—Days after the image of the crucified Christ spoke to him at the falling down San Damiano church, calling him by name, *"Francis, rebuild my church,"* he went off alone into the hills of Mount Subasio. Could he believe what he had heard? Did Jesus really speak to him, call him by name? He had had dreams before, to be a knight for the lord, to have a palace of knights errant serving a beautiful lady. He had gone off to war, been taken captive and ransomed a broken man. How much more can a person take? Then there had been this strange encounter with the leper a few days before, and he now wanted to be with the lepers and care for them. But the eyes of Jesus as He hung on the cross in the San Damiano church burned in his memory. Those eyes were so gentle and loving. Francis prayed, *"Lord, if I can but place my heart in your loving sight in all that I do, I will rebuild your church."*

3. The Demand of Love—Only the experience of love can be proof of love. To love, to trust, to reach into the unknown is the great daring adventure. How can we find God's love? My faith is a response to God's call to me by name, but that faith is only brought to me by the faith of others. Then through their eyes I can see the loving eyes of Jesus calling to me by name. Who are those that have looked upon me with God's eyes of love? To whom do I owe my faith in my God?

SAINT THOMAS

PEACE IN UNION WITH THE FAITHFUL

*Eight days later the disciples were in the room
and Thomas was with them.* —JOHN 20:26

1. Peace Be with You—For eight days Jesus did not return to the disciples, nor did He seek out Thomas in his solitude. It was not until Thomas either found the desire to return to his friends or was coerced to join them. Tincture of time can heal wounds of the heart, and the unbearable onslaught of grief by Thomas had dulled its pain. Thomas was with those closest to Jesus when He came in and stood among them. *"Peace be with you,"* He said. Those very words by Jesus were surely familiar to Thomas and was proof enough for Him. He found his peace in union with those he loved. The peace that Jesus brought.

2. Peace with Us—A familiar legend of Saint Francis and his little brothers is of public preaching. According to the story, Francis had the brothers process through a town, around the fountain, and out of the town in silence in response to the brothers' request to preach to the people. Upon leaving the town Francis was asked by the brothers, *"So, when shall we preach?"* And his response, *"You just did."* The very presence of those that are faithful to the message of Jesus' peace and proclaim that message by their lives speaks volumes and can be far more effective in proclaiming God's peace than the most eloquent sermon.

3. Peace Is the Highest Proof—The highest proof that we can offer to the world of Jesus' message of peace and His abiding presence among us is not of the senses or of words or manifestations, but of spiritual being in union with others. We best manifest our spiritual beliefs when our spirit resonates with the spirit of others. In that resonance, we play a symphony that the world hears and will listen to due to its overpowering presence. That communal spirit is ageless and is expressed in the Communion of Saints. The communal life of the Church is proof to the world of the Risen Lord. What is impossible alone is fulfilled in the many.

SAINT THOMAS

RESCUED

Be not faithless, but faithful. —JOHN 20:27

1. Rescued by Friends—Thomas had been in danger of losing his faith in Jesus, but he was rescued by his friends. They did not give up on him but persevered in bringing him back to them and to faith in Jesus. Upon seeing and hearing Jesus, Thomas' faith was restored, and his spirit leaped forward in even greater joy and love at receiving back what had been lost. Jesus, being fully aware of the road ahead, the rejection that they would receive from others, their trials and hardships, rebuked Thomas and gave warning to all to remain faithful.

2. Living Stones—The way that Saint Francis chose was dangerous and he may well have lost his way if it were not for his Order of Lesser Brothers, an order founded on Jesus Christ and built of living stones gathered from every part of the world. It was built as a dwelling place where the spirits of many can grow and flourish in devout love for God and one another. These were the new disciples of Jesus that would sustain and nourish and support one another. The faith of the many gives strength to the faith of the one, and the faith of the one can be the wellspring of enthusiasm to the many.

3. Signposts—The road of faith is not easily traveled alone. There are dangers on life's path and often, in spite of our best intentions, we stumble or take a wrong turn. That is why community is vital to remaining faithful. Those who travel life's way with us help us to read the signposts and can be living signposts to us. Spiritual life is a growth. It cannot be lifeless. To remain spiritually stationary is impossible. A soul that is rich in friends of God is rich in the nourishment to grow and prosper and multiply. Who are my living stones to show me the way and to strengthen me for the journey?

SAINT THOMAS

SURRENDER TO LOVE

My Lord and my God. —JOHN 20:28

1. Thomas Surrendered—The suffering of lost love and self-imposed solitude enabled Thomas to spring free of the bonds of human reason and to tenaciously embrace the discovered divinity of Jesus Christ. His cry of faith, *"My Lord and my God"* may well have gone beyond the spiritual perception of the others. Thomas not only accepted the fact of Jesus' human resurrection and His oneness with God, but carried him to adoration as being his Lord and God. Maybe at that point, all in the room grasped the divine wonder and fell to their knees in adoration and loving worship of Jesus truly now fully understood as the Son of God made man.

2. Francis Surrendered—Francis had carried the suffering of Jesus on the cross with him ever since that day in San Damiano when Jesus spoke to him from the icon. Oh, since then how he had contemplated the suffering of Jesus and longed to have been with Him beneath the cross! In preparation for the Feast of Saint Michael the Archangel, Francis journeyed to his holy mountain retreat of La Verna. On that long trek from Assisi to La Verna, Francis would think of Jesus' climb up the Mount of Calvary, and he prayed with hope-filled fear to allow him to experience the love-filled suffering of Jesus. On that mountain, Francis drew off, standing alone away from the others, and was buried in the crevice of rock. There, his heart was likewise buried deep in the soul of Jesus. Francis, like Thomas, was before the resurrected Jesus the Christ. With Jesus, on wounded feet, with outstretched and wounded hands and His pierced chest exposed, Francis sprung free from human experience and cried out, *"My Lord and my God."*

3. My Surrender—*"I am the Lord thy God"* is the command, but who can say I know the God of all majesty, the creator of the universe? It is impossible. But if we embrace Jesus, we know the Father that sent Him. Do I surrender to Jesus as the possessor of my soul and my being, the prime motive of all of my actions and desires? To kneel in adoration before God, to surrender completely to Jesus is to be my final act of love. To say deep in my soul, *"My Lord and my God"* is all that is needed to truly know God and to experience the person of Jesus.

SAINT THOMAS

BECAUSE YOU HAVE SEEN

"Happy are those that have not seen
and yet believe. —JOHN 20:29

1. Thomas Believed—Saint Thomas asked for visible proof and it was granted by Jesus; but without the love and trust of his friends, Thomas could not have given himself completely in his unique act of total surrender to his Lord and God. An act of simple faith would have brought Saint Thomas to the same end through the grace of God, but he had not learned from the experience of others to trust and put his faith in the hands of others.

2. Francis Believed—The first of the lesser brothers to join Francis was Brother Bernard of Quintavalle. Bernard had spent a night pretending to be asleep, watching Francis at prayer, and in the morning Bernard resolved to give away his wealth and to follow Francis in following Jesus. Francis had asked for companions that would, with him, follow the gospel message to give his possessions to the poor, to take nothing for the journey and to renounce self in taking up the cross to follow Jesus. Francis could not have been assured that he was, in fact, following the way of Jesus had he not had companions along the way to share his dream, to carry the cross of God's peace and to be an instrument of good in harmony with his brothers. Happy were Francis and Bernard and all the lesser brothers and poor sisters that had not seen and yet believed.

3. Reason for My Belief—What is the basis of my belief? Is it based on proof, physical reality and miracles, or intellectual conviction? Or, am I willing to accept the blessings of God as manifestations of His presence in my life? Have I trusted in the experiences of others to reinforce the blessed presence of the risen Jesus Christ in my being? Who are the Brother Bernards in my life who have been the answer to my prayers, been the inspiration to continue to follow the way even amid my doubts? Happy are those who have seen the hand of God in the everyday blessings and believed.

CHRIST THE KING

Pilate asked, "Are you the king of the Jews?" —JOHN 18:33

1. The World's Power—Pilate was a general of Rome; the power of the world. As a general, Pilate would assess the strength of his adversary. So, on that day, when Pilate asked the question, he measured the strength that Jesus could bring to bear. To Pilate, strength was measured in military might, political power, control over others, and domination of the other's will. To the world, power is proved by violence, but violence only begets violence. The world continues to demonstrate that truth. For Jesus, His strength was as a servant to His Father and to His Father's flock. His desire was to be the good shepherd, not the king of a conquering army. Jesus showed His strength when He knelt to wash feet, to bless and break bread, to feed the hungry, to cure the leper, and bring comfort to the oppressed.

2. The World's Peace—Jesus' kingdom was not of Rome's world, but Jesus left it for His followers to be instruments of peace to bring God's kingdom to this world. Nearly 800 years ago, during the fourth crusade, Francis of Assisi and Brother Illuminato came ashore in Damietta near the mouth of the Nile River to seek the sultan, the leader of the Muslim army in conflict with the Church's army. The fact that Francis and Illuminato returned alive attests that Francis sought neither to conquer nor to convert the sultan. Surely Francis went to the sultan, as we pray today, to be an instrument of peace, to seek to understand, to sow love where there is only hatred, to bring light and hope where there is only sadness and despair.

3. God's Peace—To be and to go in God's peace is what we are to seek for ourselves, for others, and for the people of all nations. This is to be our prime objective regardless of how others view God or by what name they pray to God. We can only wonder what peace has been won in the world by the multitude of gentle souls who fasted and prayed and may have accepted abuse and death rather than to take up the sword against others. Maybe to finally achieve God's kingdom on this earth there will be a vast army of peace-loving beggars to be instruments of peace to outweigh the forces of hatred and violence. Such was the example of Jesus and the dream of Francis. It is but for me to add my prayer and my goodwill to that army of God's peace.

SING PRAISES OF GOD

Suddenly with the angel there was a great throng of the
heavenly host, praising God and singing. —LUKE 2:13

1. Angels Sang God's Praises—At Jesus' birth an angel came to the shepherds
   announcing the good news of His birth in Bethlehem. Suddenly, many
   angels appeared and sang the praises of God. What had been known in
   heaven was now announced on earth—Jesus, the Son of God, had come to
   the world. What had been mere rock and earthen matter supporting plant
   and animal life that withered and died in an instant of eternity was now
   blessed and sanctified by God's presence among mankind. God's grace, the
   grace of His Son, would change the world and would bring God's peace
   to let us spring free from the mortal bonds of earth.

2. Francis Sang God's Praises—While on Mount La Verna and after receiving the message from the Seraph and the stigmata of Jesus' wounds on his
   body, he composed *The Praises of God*. How like the angels in Bethlehem
   almost 1,200 years earlier, at the intimate coming of Jesus to His earthly
   dwelling, Francis burst forth in praises of the holy Lord God who does
   wonderful things. With the grace of God, Francis could proclaim the many
   names of God unto the goodness and sweetness of our God.

3. We Are to Sing God's Praises—Whether the angels in heaven or the saints
   on earth, we are all to praise our God. If nothing else, and at its minimum,
   we are to praise God by giving thanks for the many blessings with which
   God graces us. Do I daily thank God? Do I count my many blessings? Is
   there someone in my life, my angel, that brings good news to me of the
   presence and praises of God? Do I thank others for reminding me of the
   sweetness of God and His saving grace? Do it; it matters.

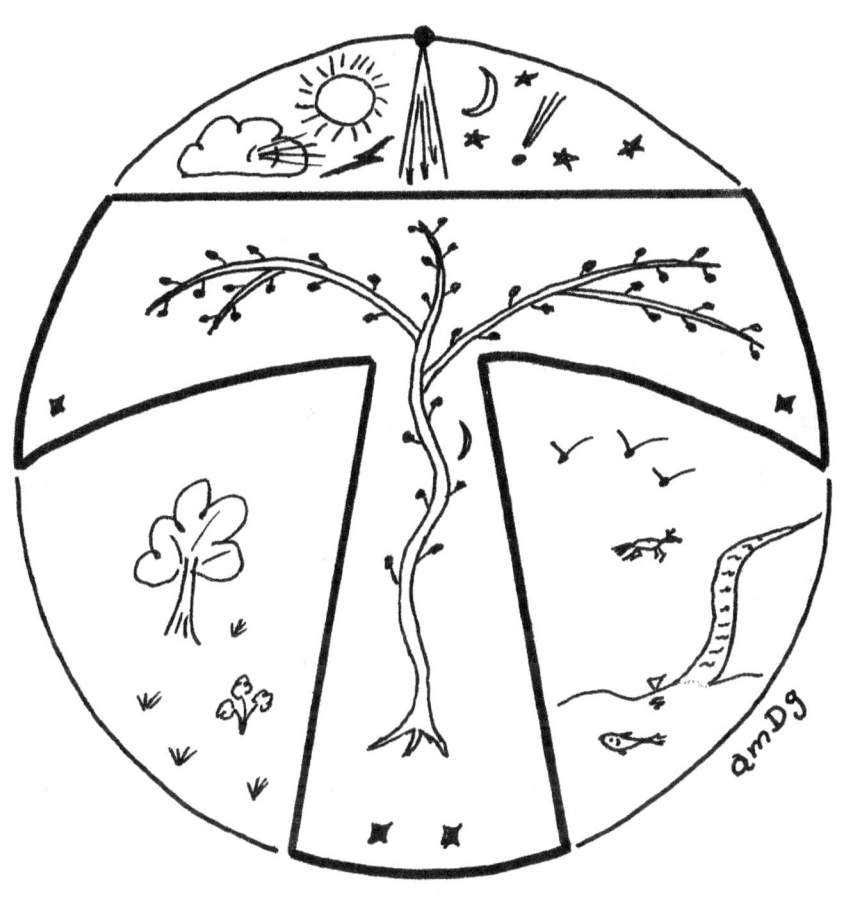

Jesus Takes His Cross by Kevin Novack

A REFLECTION OF JESUS

If anyone wants to be a follower of mine, let him renounce
himself and take up his cross and follow me. —Matt 16:24

1. Christ Is the Pattern—If there are words of Jesus in the gospels that are
   difficult to understand and hard to embrace, these surely rank among
   the most challenging. If, as a condition to be a follower of Christ means
   to renounce our self and to embrace our cross, then there may well be
   but a few that can follow Jesus into the Kingdom. Some may find this a
   riddle for how might one save his life by losing it. Jesus presents Himself
   as the pattern of God's way, not the world's or mankind's way, a pattern
   to be measured as a reflection of Jesus and the love of the Father: to be an
   instrument of peace through the grace of the Holy Spirit.

2. Francis Is a Reflection—Saint Francis is but a reflection of Jesus. For nearly
   800 years his manner of living has shown forth as an example to others,
   for he carried not only his cross, but more importantly, he carried Jesus in
   his heart through divine love that lit up a dark and dreary world. He gave
   birth to Jesus by his manner of living, and he did the will of the Father
   in heaven. In all that Francis was, he desired to bear Jesus to everyone he
   encountered, from the leper to the pope, from the beggar to the sultan,
   from the wolf to the children of Gubbio. This is the example that Francis
   gives today. To renew our lives and to reflect Jesus and the love of God
   the Father. To be an instrument of peace to all through the saving grace
   of the Holy Spirit.

3. My Reflection of Jesus—Jesus set a condition to be "His follower." As
   the cross of Jesus cannot be our cross, we can be but a reflection of Him.
   How we satisfy that condition will depend on the extent that we answer
   the call to do the will of the Father and through the graces that we are
   given by the Holy Spirit to carry out God's will. We will not be called as
   Francis was called, but we have the abundant grace to be a clear reflection
   of Jesus as we are called in this life.

THE SEA OF TIBERIUS

SACRED TIME, SACRED PLACES

> Simon Peter said, "I'm going fishing." They
> replied, "We'll come with you." —JOHN 21:3

1. Sacred Time—In obedience to the word of the risen Jesus, the disciples left Jerusalem and returned to Galilee. Time was given to them to recall the way with Jesus. The old scenery, the memories, nothing was to be forgotten. But now they were to see and learn to understand all that had happened to them in light of their new experience, their new reality of Jesus the Christ of God. The wait was long and uncertain, and Peter returned to what he knew, fishing, and others joined him. But they were not to return to their previous existence. Failure awaited them and, in that failure, they would be open to God's opportunity of a lifetime for them. They would be fishers of men and women.

2. Sacred Places—For more than 20 years, as Francis and his brothers ventured out bringing the living word of God into the world, they always found sustenance in returning to Assisi, to the Portiuncula and to their beloved Mount Subasio. For Francis, every return would be filled with memories of his escape to the caves of Mount Subasio where he could free himself from the loneliness of the city and find comfort in his growing dependence on Jesus. His heart surely leaped with joy as he would return to the chapel of San Damiano. Although Francis and Clare would always have the memory of each other carried within their hearts and souls, how their spirits would soar with the larks knowing that only the walls of San Damiano separated them. How often did those sacred memories call Francis to return to his previous way? But, like Peter, those sacred memories were but a reminder that the Lord had also called Francis and Clare and their followers; that they, too, were to be fishers of men and women for God.

3. Our Sacred Places and Memories—The places and times that speak to us of our God and our relation to Him are our greatest treasurers. How often have we stood in the same place and recalled a time when we felt the presence of God? Sacred places are like dear friends; they know our joys, our triumphs, our sorrows and our failures. Those places are made beautiful to us in the interpretation that they have given to our lives. What places, what times do we wish to recall that cause our spirits to soar to God? They are there for us to recall the path that we are called to by our Lord. What reminds us that we, too, in our way, like Peter and Francis, are also called to be fishers of men and women?

THE SEA OF TIBERIUS

JESUS ON THE SHORE

Jesus called out, "Have you caught
anything, friends?" —JOHN 21:5

1. Jesus Worked through the Night—While Peter and some of the fishermen apostles were on Lake Tiberius fishing, Jesus was on the shore. He had prepared a fire with fish and bread for those that He called friends. It is so like Jesus. How many times He had fed His friends; in the upper room, on the mound, at Emmaus, surely on the road many times. Again, Jesus, the son of man, the son of Mary and Joseph, the Son of God reached out His hands in preparation for the needs of others. It is to be expected, now as before, Jesus continues to work through the night of our struggles to feed us and care for us in the dawn of a new day.

2. Jesus Waited at San Damiano—Like Peter finding refuge on the water of Lake Tiberius, Francis found refuge at San Damiano. How often Francis had prayed before the icon of the crucified Christ at San Damiano is unknown, but surely he found comfort there in his time of loneliness, doubt and searching. Jesus' blessing and call to Francis was veiled at first. It took time for Francis to see deep into the icon and into Jesus' eyes truly looking back at him. Then Jesus, like at Lake Tiberius, was able to call to Francis and ask him the same question, *"Have you caught anything, friend?"* Maybe that was when Francis could admit that his searching had netted no catch. Francis was then ready to net Jesus' catch of a lifetime. Jesus had waited patiently on the shore of San Damiano for Francis and was ready to feed and comfort him by the fire of everlasting love.

3. Jesus Waits Patiently for Us—Peter and the disciples were occupied with their life's work. Francis was at prayer. God chooses the time and the place, but surely, He comes to each of us. The presence and blessing of God may be veiled at first; we don't see or recognize Him but surely He is at work. The knowledge of God and the call of Jesus may come slowly to the mind, but it comes if we look and wait patiently.

THE SEA OF TIBERIUS

CONVICTION

The disciple Jesus loved said to Peter, "It is the Lord." —JOHN 21:5

1. John and Peter—It was John who first recognized that it was Jesus on the shore, and he shared that with his friend Peter. For John, the repetition of events, fishing on the lake, the night of fruitless toil, the call from the shore to lower the nets to the other side, all pointed to none other than Jesus. It was Jesus' way and John knew it in an instant. We can imagine John grasping Peter by the shoulders and exclaiming his newfound discovery of Jesus all over again. What joy there was for John in telling his friend and what joy there was for Peter and the disciples to receive the good news.

2. Clare and Agnes—The world was like the Sea of Tiberius to Francis and his brothers. There were many fish to catch, and that meant lowering the net in many places. Agnes knew of Francis and Clare from the early Franciscan brothers who ventured to Prague in Bohemia. From her castle, Agnes rejected the offers of marriage from the kings of Germany and England, but rather took the hand of Jesus. She had a church, a friary and a monastery with a hospital built for the poor. Within a few years she entered the monastery to live as Clare lived with the Poor Ladies of San Damiano. Although Clare and Agnes never met, they exchanged letters. How like John and Peter in the boat, each sharing with the other the joy in discovering Jesus waiting for them with sustenance and comfort and love. For Clare and Agnes, everything pointed to Jesus, and they would find joy in pointing to Jesus for all to see and hear throughout the world for all ages.

3. Jesus Still Serves—Jesus still waits on the shore for me. Jesus, the Son of God, is a God who serves. His goal is to be recognized. All nature, all of life points to Him. With God's grace and my acceptance, I will see Jesus. He waits for me, He calls to me. It is not enough to recognize Him and to go to Him. I must embrace others with my joy and point to Jesus for others to find Him. There is a grace for every person to find Jesus. There is a greater grace to point to Jesus for others. What good do I make of those graces?

THE SEA OF TIBERIUS

JESUS' CALL TO ACTION

Jesus said, "Bring some of the fish you
have just caught." —JOHN 21:10

1. Peter Acts—At Jesus' request, Peter acts. He goes to the boat and drags the net to shore. There are 153 big fish and the net does not break. How like the event when Jesus first called to them on the lake; then the net threatened to break, but not now. Then they were not ready for the Lord's work; they could break under the load then, but not so now. They had been strengthened, they had been fed, and the Lord will continue to strengthen and feed them with His bread, with His wine. As Peter had once broken under the load, there is no longer a fear of breaking.

2. Francis Acts—How many times had Francis seen lepers? Maybe during daylight within the walls of Assisi begging for food or outside of the city living in squalor and separation from all that they had known. For they were the living dead. Each time that he came upon lepers, even within his sight, he turned and fled from them. His body, his mind, his spirit, his very being would break and he would retreat in fear and repulsion. What was it that one time, the first of many times, to be drawn by compassion, to bear up and not break, to not only reach out but to cling to and embrace what previously had been bitter but now was sweetness to Francis? The scenes were the same: the startled recognition the same, the putrid smell of rotting flesh the same. Now he was ready for his work which was to be the Lord's work through him. With that one startling act, the Lord, through Francis, could start a worldwide movement to turn bitterness to sweetness.

3. My Acts—As Jesus acted and gave of Himself on the cross, as Peter and the disciples acted and gave themselves for countless souls, as Francis and Clare and the Franciscan brotherhood and sisterhood have given of themselves throughout the world, so are we called to act and to give. It is ours to accept or to refuse. What bounty is to be had if we choose wisely?

THE SEA OF TIBERIUS

THE TEST OF LOVE

*Then Jesus said a third time, "Simon son of
John, do you love me?" —JOHN 21:17*

1. Peter's Test—Not only did Jesus put Peter to the test three times, but He
   also called Peter by his name when first they met, Simon the son of John.
   It is a twofold test, both a test of his affirmation of love but also a test of
   whether Peter had the faith and courage to be the fisher of men that Jesus
   had called him to be. Or would he rather return to his previous existence
   as Simon the fisherman? The repeated question was made for Peter to fully
   grasp what loving Jesus without reservation was to mean. Peter needed to
   love with a courage that would shrink from nothing, casting out all fear,
   for he would no longer be a fisherman but a shepherd, and a shepherd
   must tend the flock with no fear.

2. Francis' Test—The rapidity which the Order of Lesser Brothers grew is
   remarkable. Soon there were hundreds, then thousands, of men, including
   many priests who sought to follow Francis' way of life. That growth, that
   diversity of thought brought challenges to Francis and the order. How was
   poverty to be defined, how to be lived? And what did it really mean to want
   nothing? Was there not now a need for buildings and property to support
   Christ's growing army working throughout the world? The questions, the
   organizational challenges bore heavy upon Francis. As the questions rose
   again and again, Francis clung tenaciously and courageously to the word
   of the Lord that he had received, but also with loving compassion for his
   brothers that they, too, may hear the Lord with the same spirit but different words for them. For the good shepherd, his courage and lack of fear
   never outpaces his tender care for the lambs of the flock.

3. Our Test—To be a true follower of Christ, one's life cannot be one's own.
   For the Christian, the calling is to be a worker for Christ. The lambs need
   feeding, the sheep need tending. For what have I been called? Do I have
   the courage to answer the call? Do I love Jesus enough to work for Him
   even when challenged, even when unnoticed by those closest to me?

THE SEA OF TIBERIUS

Letting Go

After this Jesus said, "Follow me." —John 21:19

1. Peter Let Go—With those words, *follow me*, Peter's freedom was freely given. Hereafter Peter was bound by grace to Jesus the Christ. His previous life's freedom, as a youth, as a fisherman, as a follower of Jesus were no longer. The binding was completed with Peter's threefold declaration of his love. Now Peter was to feed God's sheep, tend God's lambs. His life was no longer his, it belonged to others. From now on, everything was in Jesus' hands, bound with the rope of love and tied with the knot of grace.

2. Clare Let Go—Francis' words had brought Clare to a reality of the love of God that no one else had been able to do, a divine love, like Peter's, that bound her to the Lord. But to be bound to the Lord meant letting go of all else. First, she let go of all that she knew: her family, her position, her possessions. That was easy because Francis was there to take her hand. Her heart pounded with love that Palm Sunday night at the Portiuncula with Francis and the brothers. This was all that she could ask of life, to be in love with God and to be with those who loved God as she did. Then Clare had to let go of that which was dearest in this life, to be separated from Francis. God's love brought them together, and God's love separated them from one another all their lives. How often did Clare and Francis cry out to God, *"Lord you know everything, you know I love you."*

3. Love Demands All—We are all to be bound to God with the rope of love and the knot of grace. Whatever path we are on in this life, we are all called to work with the Lord and to do His work. Who are those who have supported us as we let go to truly love? Who are those who we need to reach out to and to show God's love? What is it in my life that I must let go? Can I, like Peter and Clare, say through it all, *"Lord you know I love you."*

THE SEA OF TIBERIUS

SACRED EXPECTATION

And Jesus said, "Watch out then, because you do
not know the day or the hour." —MATT 25:13

1. The Kingdom of Heaven—Jesus used the parable of the ten girls with
    lamps waiting for the bridegroom to tell how we are to expect the kingdom
    of heaven. We are to be prepared for the kingdom for surely it will come,
    just as the child Jesus came to the world in Bethlehem. The world was not
    prepared then nor did it expect God, the savior of the world, to arrive in
    humility, weakness, and dependence upon a human mother and a protect-
    ing father. While men slept, Jesus was born, and the world was changed.

2. Francis and Clare Waited—Long did Francis wait to awake from his dream,
    his dream to be a knight for a powerful lord. Francis waited and listened and
    watched for the signs of the Lord's coming. Like the five wise girls, Francis
    made himself ready as he waited. How long was it that Clare waited to
    join Francis? For years she saw Francis in the streets of Assisi, heard him
    preach in the churches of San Ruffino and San Giorgio. Did she talk to
    Guido, the bishop of Assisi, and tell him of her wait to serve God, of her
    desire to follow Jesus as Francis did? Francis and Clare, neither knowing
    the journey before them, neither knowing how God would come to them,
    kept their lamp burning before the Lord. The lamp was replenished with
    the oil of prayer; the wick of their devotion was trimmed with the Holy
    Eucharist. If they were to wait, and wait they did, they would be found
    ready when the Lord came. They were not asleep when Jesus came, and
    the world was changed.

3. Our Lamp—We are to have our lamp of expectation lit. We do not know
    the day or the hour when the Lord will come to us, when we will be called
    to serve the kingdom of God. What is our calling? We may not know, but
    the Father knows. At the right hour, in the right place, we will be told.
    Be prepared by giving thanks each day. Each day is a new blessing, a step
    closer to where we are to be. Return each day in prayer, in adoration and
    thanksgiving. If so, we will be ready, and our world will be changed.

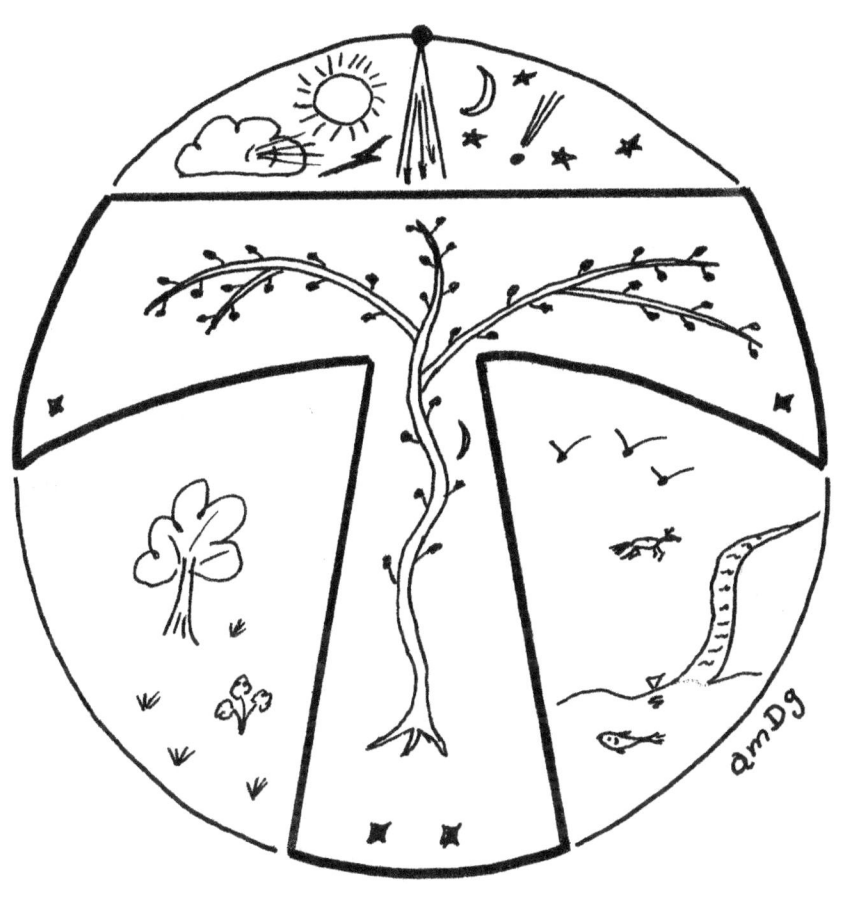

The Leper's Hand by Esther Stewart

> She said to herself, "If I can only touch His
> cloak I shall be well again." —Matt 9:21

1. To Touch Jesus—The woman with a hemorrhage had suffered for twelve years. No one and nothing that she tried had cured her. She was ceremonially unclean and had no recourse left. She knew of Jesus, maybe heard Him speak, and surely she knew of His cures of others. She came behind Him, reached out her hand and touched the fringe of His cloak. With that, she hoped to be healed, and was.

2. Touched by the Leper—The man had suffered for many years with the scourge of leprosy. There was no cure. He had been stripped of his dignity as a living human being, his possessions had been taken from him, and he was declared dead to his family, society and the Church. There was nothing left for him. Hope had long been lost. Only the relief of death remained. He walked the road alone in his misery. Turning the corner, he was confronted by a man on a horse. Francis would normally turn and run in terror at the mere sight of a leper, but not this time. For Francis and the leper, time, life, and souls stood still. Francis' dream! To be a knight for the Lord, to go where others trembled in fear, to right the wrong, to win the hand of the lady. Lady Poverty was there in her terrible disguise. Francis sprang from his horse, rushed to the leper and threw his arms around him. Embracing him, he kissed him. Again, time stood still. With tears of joy both withdrew. Francis mounted and rode on. Numb with mercy, Francis turned and the leper was gone.

3. Awakened by Touch—Human suffering thronged Jesus in His earthly ministry. For Francis, his last desire was to return to his ministry to the lepers. Human suffering has always existed in this world. Jesus brought the spirit of compassionate touch to heal humanity. To bring hope where there was suffering and light where there was darkness, Saint Francis, in following and always pointing to Jesus, renewed the spirit of mankind to the compassion of Jesus and awoke the world to the loving mercy of an all-good God the Father. How do I respond to the touch of others? I, too, am to be like Francis and awaken the world to an all-good God.

INDEX OF NAMES

INDEX OF NAMES

INDEX OF PLACES

INDEX OF PLACES

INDEX OF KEYWORDS

INDEX OF SCRIPTURE CITATIONS

INDEX OF SCRIPTURE CITATIONS

CITATIONS	PAGE NUMBER
John 1:1	1
John 1:-5	49
John 1:34	77
John 2:1-2	3
John 2:3-4	4
John 2:5	5
John 2:7	6
John 2:10	7
John 2:23-25	51
John 3:8	53
John 5:17	61
John 8:12	52
John 9:39	55
John 10:11	97
John 11:16	98
John 11:27	94
John 13:4-5	54
John 14:8	89
John 15:5	33
John 15:15	35
John 18:33	105
John 20:19	57
John 20:20	58
John 20:24	99
John 20:25	100
John 20:26	101
John 20:27	102
John 20:28	103
John 20:29	104
John 21:3	110
John 21:5	111, 112

INDEX OF SCRIPTURE CITATIONS

CITATIONS	PAGE NUMBER
John 21:10	113
John 21:17	114
John 21:19	115, 116
1 John 3:1	71
Psalm 127:2	98
Ezekiel 9:4	56

ABOUT THE AUTHOR

George Sabol is a member of the Secular Franciscan Order and lives in New Mexico and Arizona. He has studied at the Franciscan Institute of St. Bonaventure University in Olean, New York. He has engineering degrees from St. Louis University in St. Louis, Missouri, and from Colorado State University in Ft. Collins, Colorado. He was a member of the Civil Engineering faculty of New Mexico State University in Las Cruces, New Mexico. For more than 25 years, he has been active with the Casa Franciscana mission in Guaymas, Sonora, Mexico, and is on the board of directors for the Casa Franciscana Outreach operating out of the Franciscan Renewal Center in Scottsdale, Arizona. He has made presentations on Franciscan studies in Arizona, Colorado, and New Mexico. For more than 50 years he has worked in the United States and internationally as a water resources engineer and has numerous technical publications.

You can join him for presentations of these meditations in an oral, storytelling fashion on his podcast, "Meditations of Peace and Good" through Spotify, or through his website, georgesabol.com.

www.ingramcontent.com/pod-product-compliance
Lightning Source LLC
Chambersburg PA
CBHW060536130626
46553CB00002B/772